CHRISTIAN ENCOUNT

WILLIAM F.
BUCKLEY JR.

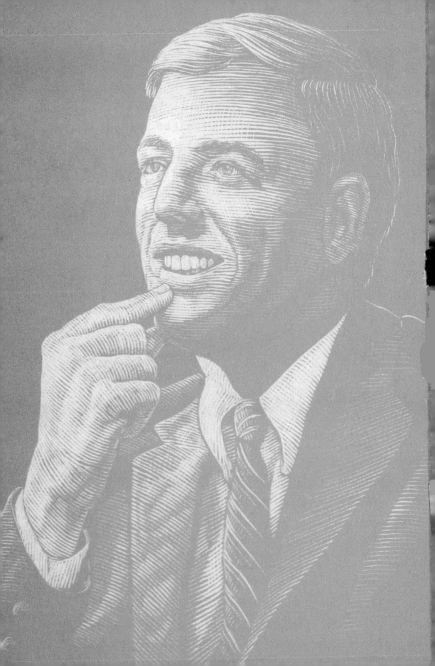

CHRISTIAN ENCOUNTERS

WILLIAM F. BUCKLEY JR.

JEREMY LOTT

THOMAS NELSON
Since 1798

NASHVILLE   DALLAS   MEXICO CITY   RIO DE JANEIRO

Published in Nashville, Tennessee, by Thomas Nelson. Thomas Nelson is a
registered trademark of Thomas Nelson, Inc.

Thomas Nelson, Inc., titles may be purchased in bulk for educational, business,
fund-raising, or sales promotional use. For information, please e-mail
SpecialMarkets@ThomasNelson.com.

Library of Congress Cataloging-in-Publication Data

Lott, Jeremy.
  William F. Buckley Jr. : Christian encounters / by Jeremy Lott.
    p. cm. — (The generals)
  Includes bibliographical references and index.
  ISBN 978-1-59555-065-1 (alk. paper)
 1. Buckley, William F. (William Frank), 1925–2008. 2. Buckley, William F.
(William Frank), 1925–2008—Religion. 3. Novelists, American—20th
century—Biography 4. Journalists—United States—Biography. I. Title.
  PS3552.U344Z76 2010
  070.92—dc22
  [B]   2010012838

Printed in the United States of America

10 11 12 13 HCI 6 5 4 3 2 1

To Andrew and, especially, Laura Lott.
Welcome to the family.

CONTENTS

"We are in danger of going mad, and I take the liberty of declaring madness to be un-American."

—William F. Buckley Jr., speech at the New Yorker Hotel, May 7, 1958

"I . . . told him that vaticide was the act of killing a prophet, and that if he wanted to go down as guilty of that crime, all he had to do was kill me."

—William F. Buckley Jr., letter to President Reagan, June 28, 1987

INTRODUCTION

SAINT BILL?

Washington DC every February is host to a conference of unlikely activists that is known by its acronym: CPAC. The conference in 2010 was held at the massive Marriott Wardman Park Hotel. Approximately ten thousand attendees listened to speeches over three days by presidential hopefuls, other politicians, and pundits; took in breakaway sessions and rallies; got out to see some sights around DC; and partied late into the night.

The thing that makes CPAC odd is that its activist attendees are . . . conservatives. You wouldn't necessarily know that from looking at them. Every CPAC includes thousands of college students, slightly older folks from all over the country in all walks of life, and representatives of a wide array of organizations that want to reach these conservatives—from representatives of think tanks to hawkers of knickknacks. (I picked up a pro-life Slinky at the 2010 convention and a copy of *Grandma's Not Shovel-Ready*, a book of photographs of protest signs.)

People aren't quite sure what to make of CPAC. Every year, journalists go to gawk. Regulars and employees of the local restaurants can't quite understand it either. On the one hand, they crack jokes about the vast right-wing conspiracy here in our midst. On the other hand, that posture is rather hard to maintain when all of these conservatives are sitting in public restaurants, with name tags hung around their necks, talking openly—and often excitedly—about speeches and ideas.

William F. Buckley Jr. made this all possible, and he hasn't really left the building. His first serious biographer, John Judis, bestowed on Buckley the title "Patron Saint of the Conservatives," and that has become truer now, after Buckley's passing, than in his life. He founded a movement that has outlived him, and in some ways embodies him.

Before the 2010 CPAC, a group of conservative graybeards released the Mount Vernon Statement, a declaration about the future of the movement. At the convention, when people discussed it, they often talked about how inferior it was to the Sharon Statement that Buckley had had a hand in—way back in 1960.

Buckley in life was a Catholic, and in that capacity he will never be declared a saint. He was too political a figure to pull that trick off. But he won't go away because Judis was onto something.

People keep coming back to Buckley for a reason, though they don't know why exactly. They point to his arguments, his wit, his wisdom. But this book will argue that they are missing something. Buckley's arguments and his politics were inspired and bounded by his religion.

ATHWART CONSENSUS

Buckley's religion is what made him truly interesting because it brought him into sharp conflict with too many people to count. He tangled with moderate Republicans, lukewarm liberal academics, Communists, anti-anti-Communists, Objectivists, Protestants, anti-Semites, progressive and traditionalist Catholics. Some of those fights he went looking for. Others found him. But he was often shocked by the ferocity of the responses he provoked.

That was naïve on Buckley's part. He should have seen it coming. From the moment he appeared on the national scene with his first book, *God and Man at Yale*, he played a role that always disturbs the peace: the role of prophet. Buckley pitched himself as a modern Jonah, warning of the doom to come if America didn't change course, quickly. He stood as a living, breathing, grinning, eyebrow-arching rebuke to more than one national consensus.

These agreements included the liberal consensus in academia, the Cold War consensus to perhaps contain but not roll back advances by Communist countries, the domestic consensus in favor of what was left of the New Deal, the growing cultural consensus in favor of greater experimentation unmoored from tradition, and the social consensus that religion and politics are private things that we do not discuss in polite company. Buckley tried to sweep these all away into history's dustbin.

But first he needed a broom. So he set about to do something about that. He fashioned the modern conservative movement out of materials of various American passions and movements left lying around. Many scholars and handicappers of all political stripes have looked at the rise of conservatism in America and said the same thing, or near enough the same thing: Buckley made it possible. George Nash, the preeminent historian of postwar conservatism, said that Buckley "changed minds, he changed lives, and he helped to change the direction of American politics."[1]

Patrick Allitt, Nash's nearest rival, explained that Buckley's "aim was to set up a big tent, bringing in as many types of conservatives as possible, and keep them together despite their differences."[2] We can't say for sure that someone else wouldn't have come along and assembled a new movement that would eventually turn American politics on its ear. We can say that the person who actually did so was Buckley.

In fact, "conservative" and "liberal" mean very different things now than they did before Bill Buckley went to work. "Liberal" simply meant generous or broadminded, socially. To say that Bob Smith was a man of liberal opinion was to say that he was a learned and good man. Politically, liberalism had begun as a philosophy of human liberation that focused on changing society by changing laws.

Liberals opposed human bondage and government restraints on trade, speech, and religion. Philosophers Adam Smith, John

Locke, and John Stuart Mill—the leading theorists behind the invisible hand, political toleration, and freedom of speech—were liberals, all. People who wish to draw on their example call themselves "classical liberals."

There are two reasons why that "classical" hedge is now necessary, at least in the United States. The first is that the Progressive movement of the late nineteenth and early twentieth centuries made a huge dent on public opinion. Though many opponents of President Franklin Delano Roosevelt's policies in the 1930s considered themselves liberals, people who advocated for a much stronger, larger, and quite visible hand of government also called themselves liberals. This bred confusion.

The second reason is Bill Buckley. He loathed the modern set of ideas that he called liberalism and regularly lacerated liberals as unthinking enemies of God and decency and puppies. He said they were dummies who didn't understand economics, control freaks who couldn't plan their way out of a paper bag, dupes who didn't appreciate the dangers of Communism—at home and abroad.

Booker T. Washington had called his book about the lives of black Americans after the Civil War *Up from Slavery*. Bill Buckley titled his first and only political treatise *Up from Liberalism*. In Buckley's capable rhetorical hands, liberalism became a term of derision, a taunt, a swear word. In this book we will look at how he did that and, more important, why. It won't ruin any surprises to say that Buckley viewed the conflict as ultimately religious in nature.

WHERE HAVE YOU GONE, BILL BUCKLEY?

After Bill Buckley's death in 2008, thinkers have drafted the founder of modern conservatism for a number of causes that Buckley never would have signed on to if he were still drawing breath. It began with the obits. Some on the left praised his intelligence, wit, and sophistication and contrasted it with modern conservative Neanderthalism. Message: sure, Bill Buckley was something—but his followers, whoa boy! They're something else entirely!

A few writers have even tried to conscript into their struggle against populist conservatism the man who famously said that he'd rather be governed by the first two thousand names in the Boston phone book than by the whole faculty of Harvard. *New York Times Book Review* editor Sam Tanenhaus, Buckley's official biographer, who has said that his subject's first book "contained the seeds of a movement,"[3] took time out from writing Buckley's bio to knock off a quickie book on the death of said conservatism, a death which, at this writing, looks to be greatly exaggerated.

To borrow Buckley for their causes, pundits typically must ignore the inconvenient facts right in front of their noses. Self-styled pragmatists have to ignore the fact that he loathed the mainstream Republicanism of the 1950s and set up a magazine, *National Review*, to combat it. Liberals have to ignore his liberal baiting and championing of the antichrist, Senator Joe McCarthy. Elitists must ignore his unabashed populism. Those who would use Buckley to argue for a bigger government have to pretend that he didn't have a mean libertarian streak. Name one other major candidate for mayor of New York City who ever denounced the minimum wage or rent control or compulsory unionism as immoral.

Scoundrels who employ Buckley's urbane conservatism as a bludgeon to beat the religious right have by far the most to ignore. Buckley railed against secularism on campus as the chairman of the *Yale Daily News* and began his public career by calling for the reinforcement of Christian orthodoxy at his quickly secularizing alma mater. He opposed Communism and liberalism ultimately for theological reasons. The policies that he advocated proceeded from his understanding of how society should be ordered—an understanding that was profoundly shaped by his religion. He called for an amendment to the Constitution protecting human life well before *Roe v. Wade* made abortion on demand the law of the land, for instance.

This book will not be a point-by-point refutation of the misuses of Bill Buckley, because that would be long and—Buckley's cardinal sin—boring. The idea is to present a story that contains an argument. The story is the public life of Buckley. The argument concerns the role he played, and how Buckley saw himself.

I will show, through Buckley's words and demeanor, that he sometimes saw himself as something of a prophet. He took to this mode easily enough because he was a very Old Testament sort of believer. Buckley remarked that if it could ever be conclusively proved that the Resurrection never happened, then he would have no choice but to . . . become a Jew. He explained: he would still believe in the divine law handed down at Mount Sinai, so really, what other option would he have?

PROPHET A MAN

I do not believe a prophetic interpretation of Bill Buckley's life is a great stretch, though it could be overdone. Think of this as an additional layer of how to think about a public figure whose legacy endures. I will, in due course, show readers why it makes good sense to think of Buckley that way. But first a few words about what a prophet is. In the Hebrew tradition, prophets were God's mouthpieces.

Prophets spoke in a number of different ways, always calling people back to the One True Path. They warned the children of Israel, or the children of other nations, to repent, to establish a more just order, or to gird up their loins and ready themselves for the consequences. If we think of God as an irritable parent, prophets were His way of saying, "Don't make Me come down there."

Prophets are caricatured as dour one-noters. Think of camel-hair-sporting John the Baptist–types railing in the wilderness, or that entire alley full of doom-and-gloom crazy preachers in the Monty Python film *Life of Brian*. Yet prophets communicated the messages they had been sent to deliver in a startling number of ways. They preached and they prodded; they spoke to those in power and directly to the people; they acted out; they took faithless wives and called down fire from heaven; they made detailed predictions about the future; they ranted (Merriam-Webster's: "jeremiad, noun: a prolonged lamentation or complaint; *also*: a cautionary or angry harangue") and reasoned and ridiculed. Cassandra's tragedy does not stack up against Jonah's disgust, Daniel's visions, Hosea's anguish.

Kings often kept prophets on retainers, but those prophets don't tend to be remembered fondly. In 850 BC, Israel's King Ahab brought in four hundred house prophets who told him unanimously to go ahead and attack a desired military target. His ally, Judah's King Jehoshaphat, asked if they might get a second opinion from a "prophet of the Lord."

Ahab's response was telling: "There is yet one man by whom we may inquire of Yahweh, but I hate him! He never prophesies good to me, but always evil." That prophet's name was Micah. He was summoned and told the king and his court, "Do not do this thing; go home in peace instead." Micah was thrown into prison for his troubles but was proved right when Ahab was killed in battle and Israel routed.[4]

Many Christians—with a greater concentration among Protestants, and especially evangelicals—look at the details of prophecy as a way of proving that the Bible is true in every particular. I won't argue with that approach, but the larger picture is much more important to this present work. Prophets are remembered not because they were right about everything but because they were right about the things that mattered most, and set out to warn people against ruin and folly.

That is the sense in which Bill Buckley played the part of prophet. He was proved right about Communism, right about academia, right about the excesses of liberalism, and right about much else, besides. And he was motivated to *inveigh* (his preferred word: "to protest strongly or attack vehemently with words; rail") against these things by his religious understanding.

That Buckley has not been seen in this way is due to our stereotypical narrowing of how we think of prophets. To begin, he was witty, and we don't think of prophets that way, though the available evidence shows that some prophets were pretty caustic and can still draw laughs. Elijah, when he was taunting the prophets of the Canaanite god Ba'al over their inability to call down fire from heaven, openly ridiculed them and their god. He said they should speak up, because maybe Ba'al was hard of hearing or out for a jog or taking a long nap or (wait for it) on the can.

More serious charges are piled against Bill Buckley that we will have to deal with here: charges that he was a bad Catholic and a racist. On the occasion of Buckley's death, Catholic reporter Mark Stricherz looked at the press write-ups for the journalism criticism Web site GetReligion.org and rapped obit writers on the knuckles. These writers had called Buckley a "conservative Catholic" when in fact he "was not a conservative Catholic, in the religious, doctrinal sense of the term," Stricherz opined, because he "opposed the wisdom of church teaching on social and political issues." The litany: "He favored decriminalizing drugs and wrote for *Playboy*. For a time, he defended southern segregationists and supported birth control."[5]

Some critics went further, calling Buckley "the primordial cafeteria Catholic."[6] These criticisms are a stretch, in roughly the same way that trying to stretch out an old tire across the Isthmus of Panama would be a stretch. Buckley was a reasonably devout Catholic for the whole of his life. He struggled to accept Church teachings that he found difficult, sometimes at great personal cost.

There is one final good objection to the idea of Buckley-as-prophet: This is not how a prophet appears. Prophets are not Yale-educated world-class debaters. They are not witty or quite so polysyllabic. They warn that the end is near if we don't repent, not that we should struggle to so as not to "eminentize the eschaton." They do not wear tweed or start magazines or run for mayor of New York. For that matter, they don't write syndicated columns or host long-running PBS shows or write spy novels either.

That may be true of prophets of old, but . . . this one did.

≈

This is a selective treatment of Buckley's life, not an exhaustive one, and I hope it will encourage readers to go back to the source material—principally Buckley's books, speeches, columns, long essays, novels, and television broadcasts. (See Recommended Reading in the Appendix at the back of the book.) Though he never wrote a formal biography, Buckley was his own best biographer, from his first book to his final reminiscence about Ronald Reagan. Buckley occasionally tried to tame the use of the first person, and failed. Even when he managed to avoid the "I," his personality is ever present. It's so strong that you get the sense he is still here with us.

1

BUCKLEYS,
NOT KENNEDYS

When sons are named for their fathers, they are often called by different names to avoid undue confusion. An angry mother doesn't want to order her son to "get down here this instant!" and accidentally summon her confused husband instead. So it was with William F. Buckley Jr. He was born on November 24, 1925, to Aloïse Steiner-Buckley and William Frank Buckley. The father was known as "Will," so the sixth of ten children became "Bill"— later, "Chairman Bill."

Bill Buckley's parents left a heavy imprint on their son's character, his politics, his religion, and his ambition. When Will Buckley died in 1958 of complications arising from an earlier stroke, Bill wrote that it was to his father's "encouragement, moral and material" that Bill's magazine *National*

Review "owes its birth and early life." Will was a Texan, a lawyer, an oilman, a self-starter, and a rebel—at one point, literally.

Will Buckley had been expelled from Mexico in 1921 for backing a failed plot against the government of that country. "The fact that the counterrevolutionaries were decent men and those in power barbarians," Bill reflected, "does not alter the political reality, which is that it is a very dangerous business indeed to back an unsuccessful insurrection—and he knew it and barely escaped with his skin."[1] Will had tried to stay out of the affairs of his host nation, but as the Mexican Revolution turned antiforeigner, anti-Catholic, and murderously anti-clerical, he felt his hand was forced.

Before the revolution things were tolerable but far from perfect for the Catholic Church in Mexico. Land-hungry regimes would sometimes confiscate Church property. There were anticlerical laws on the books—for instance, banning any Church involvement with burial grounds. But these were rarely enforced. By the time Will Buckley opened his Tampico law office in 1911, matters were worsening as the Mexican Revolution heated up. Over the next decade, he witnessed what happens when leftist revolutionaries gain power.

Plutarco Calles, while governor of Sonora, had expelled all Catholic priests from the Northwestern state (just south of Arizona), and the new Mexican revolutionary constitution of 1917 made things worse. It outlawed foreign-born priests, banned all monastic orders, deprived priests of the right to vote, seized all Church property, prohibited clergy from wearing clerical garb outside of church, and eliminated the right to a jury trial for any violation of the state's anticlerical laws. To have the state seize his neighbor's land, all a man had to do was tell the authorities that his neighbor was holding the land for the Church.

Nor did things get better for some time after Will Buckley was forced out. Before the Revolution, there were forty-five hundred priests in all of Mexico. By 1935, there were some three hundred priests in the entire country, and that was after conditions were somewhat relaxed. The rest of the priests had been killed, exiled, or harassed into leaving. When he became president in 1925, Calles made use of the laws against Church education to shutter Catholic schools and force the children into aggressively secularist state-run schools.

Things got so bad that in 1926 Pope Pius XI issued the letter *Iniquis Afflictisque* ("On the Persecution of the Church in Mexico"), which began by declaring "no hope or possibility of relief from the sad and unjust conditions under which the Catholic religion exists today in Mexico except it be by a 'special act of Divine Mercy.'"[2]

Many Mexican Catholics took that as a call to arms. One year later, the so-called Cristero War began. Catholic guerrillas staged a three-year armed uprising after years of protests and boycotts had failed to curb Calles's anticlerical, anti-Catholic policies. A truce had to be negotiated by U.S. Ambassador to Mexico Dwight Whitney Morrow.

NOT SUCH A BAD GUY

Bill wrote that his old man "never forgot his distrust of the revolutionary ideology." This distrust he passed on to his most famous son. On an episode of his *Firing Line* television show that aired in 1973, Bill had as a guest a leather-jacket-wearing, cigarette-puffing, Afro-sporting Huey Newton, cofounder of the Black Panther Party. Bill asked Newton to explain the title of his book *Revolutionary Suicide*, which led to a fascinating and unintentionally comic exchange.

NEWTON: I'll explain it, but if I may impose upon you, I have a friend who is almost dying for me to ask this question, if you will.

BUCKLEY: [*Gestures yes.*]

NEWTON: The question is, during the revolution of 1776 when the United States of America broke away from England, my friend would like to know, which side would you have been on during that time?

BUCKLEY: [*Clears throat.*] I think probably I would have been on uh, on uh, the side of George Washington. I'm not absolutely sure, because it remains to be established historically whether what we sought to prove at that point might not have been proved by more peaceful means. On the whole I'm against revolutions, but I think as revolutions go, that was a pretty humane one.

NEWTON: You're not such a bad guy after all![3]

Many Americans who witnessed the horrors of the Mexican intervention would have been tempted to call for U.S. troops to pacify their unruly neighbor. Not Will Buckley. He opposed such interventions as undue meddling by the U.S. government. He was offered the civilian governorship of Veracruz but angrily turned it down in protest of President Woodrow Wilson's decision to send troops into Europe for World War I.

Will was a fan and patron of anarchist philosopher Albert Jay Nock, author of *Our Enemy, the State*, and a member of the America First Committee, which—until the Japanese bombed Pearl Harbor—labored to keep American troops out of Europe during World War II. Bill later called his first sailboat *Sweet Isolation*, a nod to his father's politics.

Charges of cowardice, callousness, or disloyalty are often flung at America Firsters. In some particular instances those charges may be true, but by all accounts Will Buckley did not shrink from danger in Mexico. He faced the revolutionary leader and bandit Pancho Villa and talked him out of killing a trembling train conductor. He was kidnapped, threatened, and, later, exiled for his part in an attempted coup. That attempt may have been foolish, as Bill would later argue, but it showed real concern for a nation and a people that went far beyond what you would expect from a businessman looking only to enrich himself.

BANNED IN IRELAND

Will Buckley was both Irish and Catholic, but the Irish clan he hailed from had been Protestant. According to family lore, Will Buckley's grandfather (Bill's great-grandfather) had been part of the landed Protestant gentry in Cork County, Ireland. Orangemen normally paraded through his land annually to celebrate the supremacy of the English king over the Catholics of Ireland. When Buckley took a Catholic bride, he asked that his fellow Protestants not march across his land. He didn't want to disturb the missus. The Orangemen attempted to march anyway, and Buckley bloodied the first man to cross the property line—a real blow for ecumenism, you might say.

After that incident, great-grandfather Buckley felt it best to leave Ireland, and the Buckleys bounced around for generations: Canada, San Diego, Texas, Connecticut, Mexico, New York (where Bill was born on November 4, 1925), Britain, France, various points in Latin and South America. The children were educated in different languages depending on the locale at the time and the maids and tutors on hand—the sixth-born Bill spoke Spanish and French before English, for instance.

His upbringing would prepare him for a well-traveled life, with residences and serious interests in New York City and Stamford, Connecticut; a ski lodge in Switzerland, where he wrote many of his books; trips to Washington DC and other exotic locales; and frequent trips around the United States on the lecture circuit to help pay the bills for his magazine, *National Review*.

This isn't to say that the Buckleys were completely rootless. It's no accident that Bill's longest-held permanent residence was in Connecticut. Will bought an estate called Great Elm in Sharon, Connecticut, in 1923, where many of the Buckley children spent a few formative years. These were years of sailing and horse riding and other amusements for the Buckley children. Late in life, Bill tried to capture the life at Great Elm during the summers from the point of view of a young boy.

"At lunch," he wrote, "those [Buckleys] who had chosen to play golf or tennis in the morning would join the riders and we would plan the afternoon—though Mademoiselle (Mademoiselle Jeanne Bouchex, our governess) was there to see to it that no outing stood in the way of our 45 minutes required of every one of us at piano practice." For a young boy, it was heaven.

Bill was horrified to discover "nature's dirty little secret." As the summer lulled on "*the days grew shorter!*" When darkness fell at 8:30, the young Bill "wondered momentarily whether we were witnessing some sign of divine displeasure." An older brother had to explain the seasons to his distressed sibling. When Bill was forced to leave Great Elm to go to the British Jesuit boarding school St. John's Beaumont at the age of thirteen, he was nearly crushed.[4]

The Buckleys were sometimes compared to that other upwardly mobile, politically ambitious large family of Irish Catholics, the Kennedys, but hated that. The *New York Times* asked Bill to write a piece on "the Buckley Mystique," a term patterned after the then-popular phrase "the Kennedy Mystique." That subject, said his brother Reid, made Bill "acutely uncomfortable" and "made my flesh crawl also."

"We were not Kennedys," Reid wrote. "There was no 'mystique' about us at all. We were an ordinary, though large and rambunctious, American family. We had extraordinary parents, principled as no Kennedy going back to old Joe . . . ever was, inclining us to a radical dissent when it came to popular culture and to political opinions that were at the time unpopular."

Reid authored the piece instead of Bill. Though he detested the term *mystique*, Reid explained, "The *Times* was willing to pay one thousand bucks" in 1970 dollars. The upshot of his article was that "the whole point of our politics was what our parents drilled into their children: that 'God, family, and country,' *in that order*, demanded our unswerving loyalty." The Buckleys, you see, believed in classical virtues such as integrity and self-reliance. Above all, Reid said, "we were not serfs, beholden to crown or state."[5]

In contrast, the Kennedys believed in whatever was hot at that moment and would help the family advance on the national stage. They rooted for and profited from the First World War, basically sided with Hitler before Pearl Harbor, were McCarthyites when Senator Joe McCarthy was riding high, then hawkish Cold War liberals, then campaigners against the Vietnam War, which President John F. Kennedy had helped to start by sending in military advisers to Indochina. And don't get the Buckleys started on Chappaquiddick.

But there was a sense in which the comparison was all too true. Politics, for the Kennedys, were a family affair, and they tended to share the same grudges, resentments, and affections, regardless of the political pose of the moment. John F. Kennedy didn't vote for Joe McCarthy's censure. He was one of only three Democrats not to vote for censure and the only one not to go on the record deploring McCarthy. Robert F. Kennedy, who had twice served on the controversial senator's permanent Senate subcommittee, the first time at father Joe's behest, stuck up for his old boss even after the vote to condemn.

In fact, the only censure motion that JFK even entertained voting for was one that deplored McCarthy giving free reign to Roy Cohn, an aide that RFK had feuded with. When a speaker at a Harvard dinner said that he was glad JFK's alma mater had never graduated a Hiss and equally glad that it had never graduated a McCarthy, JFK famously shouted, "How *dare* you couple the name of a great American patriot with that of a traitor!"[6]

The Buckleys could be just as loyal and just as stubborn, to the point of causing a scene. When the Buckley children were at the Duchess County Horse show one year, young Patricia trotted away with the blue ribbon. President Franklin Roosevelt was in attendance, wrote Bill, and "applauded lustily, whereupon Trish abruptly turned her pigtailed head to one side." When Will Buckley asked her why she had done that to the president of the United States, his daughter professed shock: "I thought you didn't like him!"[7] She was rude but not wrong. Will loathed the president for his New Deal interventionist policies, and his kids took up their old man's grievances.

Buckley biographer John Judis offers us a different, more satisfying explanation for why the Buckleys hated being likened unto the Kennedys. The Kennedys embraced the mythology of Irish immigration with gusto. They pitched themselves as the culmination of poor outcast people's long climb up the greasy pole of American politics. Theirs was the story of a once-hated minority finally winning respect and making good. The Buckleys didn't see themselves that way at all. Their forbears had come to the United States by choice to seek greater freedom, not because of dire necessity brought on by a massive potato crop failure.

The Buckleys' Catholicism set them apart from many of their neighbors, but they were otherwise the very model of WASP refinement. They listened to classical music by the world's great composers, not Irish folk songs. And they went to school not at Notre Dame but Yale—a university that at the time would accept only so many Catholics or Jews per class.

MOTHER CHURCH, SISTER TRISH

Will Buckley was an observant but quiet Catholic with prominent Protestant ancestors. His children might—and I stress, *might*—have assimilated into some form of Protestantism if it weren't for his wife, Aloïse. She came from Swiss-German-Irish stock and grew up in Louisiana, and she inspired an intense piety in many of her children.

When the young Bill and his younger sister, Trish, found out that two guests at Great Elm were unbaptized and, thus, headed for the bad place, they sprinkled them in their sleep. They did this to several other guests until their parents found out what the kids were doing and made them knock it off.

When Aloïse died at the age of one hundred in 1985—twenty-seven years after her husband had passed away—Bill began his moving obituary of her thus: "My mother worshiped God as intensely as the saint transfixed. And his companionship to her as that of an old and very dear friend." Of her longevity he remarked, "Perhaps somewhere else one woman has walked through so many years charming so many people by her warmth and diffidence and humor and faith. If so, I wish I might have known her."

In the obituary, Bill pointed to one ugly obstacle of his youth that he would have to struggle to overcome, a genteel racism—and also to its ultimate *religious* remedy. His mother's "anxiety to do the will of God was more than ritual," Bill wrote. "The cultural coordinates of our household were Southern. But the times required that we look Southern conventions like Jim Crow hard in the face, and so I [wrote to her and] asked her how she could reconcile Christian fraternity with the separation of the races." She replied by post:

My darling Bill,

    This is not an answer to your letter, for I cannot answer it too quickly. It came this morning and, of course, I went as soon as possible to the Blessed Sacrament in our quiet beautiful little church here. And, dear Bill, I prayed so hard for humility and for wisdom and for guidance from the Holy Spirit. I know He will help me to answer your questions as He thinks they should be answered. I must pray longer before I do this.

Love, Mother [8]

Bill also inherited from his father, he would later admit while compiling a book on the subject, a mild anti-Semitism. This played no serious negative role in Bill's public career, and he was privately tolerant, mostly.

True, at his father's urging, he once talked his older sister Jane's boyfriend, Tom Guinzburg, out of proposing to her. But according to Garry Wills, when Bill finally told her what he had done, she told her brother it wouldn't have worked out anyway. Bill replied, "I wish I had known that before—I have been reproaching myself all these years." [9]

Also true: Bill threatened not to join the Yale Fence Club fraternity after they rejected Tom because he was Jewish. The frat gave in, and Tom and Bill entered together. Buckley would work very early on to purge Jew haters, and those who tolerate Jew haters, from his magazine and the growing conservative movement.

Much of what Bill would accomplish in his lifetime was helped along by his very accomplished brothers and sisters. It was fortuitous that there were so many of them. Will and

Aloïse produced ten bustling Buckley children, from 1918 to 1938, and saw to it that they had the best education possible, in the classroom and in the world. Here they are in order of birth:

1. Aloise
2. John
3. Priscilla
4. James
5. Jane
6. William
7. Patricia
8. Reid
9. Maureen
10. Carol

Readers with an ear for this sort of thing will note that most of these names do not sound very Irish. The Irish American writer Joe Queenan, who grew up in Philadelphia in the 1950s and '60s, told in his memoirs of meeting a priest with the exotic-sounding first name of "Morgan" in the mid-'60s. Queenan noted the narrow, anglicized range of names of priests that he had come across to that point.

Queenan explained that "gaudy Hibernian names like Brendan and Sean came later, when the Irish had enough money to move to the suburbs and send their kids to private schools and could afford to be more blatantly ethnic."[10] With the striving Irish upper classes, this was even more pronounced. Joseph Patrick Kennedy Sr.'s parents had been named Patrick and Bridget. After naming his first son after himself, the rest of the children took on decidedly WASP-sounding names: John, Rosemary, Kathleen, Edward, Robert, Eunice, etc.

Political observers have noted that the Kennedys tended to

die early, from fluke accidents mostly. This became an obsession in the popular press. With each death, headlines would remind us that there is a "Kennedy curse." The Buckleys' mortality rate was much lower. When Will Buckley died in 1958, all of his children were still alive. The centenarian Aloïse wasn't so lucky. Due to her longevity, she managed to outlast her first-, second-, and ninth-born children.

Her reaction to the death of her oldest son, John, months before her death, was "by her standards, convulsive," wrote Bill. But he admired the fact that she "did not break her rule—she never broke it—which was never, ever to complain; because, she explained, she could never repay God the favors He had done her, no matter what tribulations she might have to suffer."[11]

Bill Buckley's parents and upbringing show us a few of the seeds of his later success: the stubbornness, adventurousness, and entrepreneurial drive of his father; the thrill of constant activity; the means and encouragement to pursue learning; and, of course, the bedrock faith of his mother that there is a God in heaven, and everything will come out right in the end.

But in order for young Bill Buckley to become *William F. Buckley Jr.*, he had to find something that shocked his conscience. That occurred in the unlikeliest of places.

2

YALE AND GOD. OH, MAN!

God and Man at Yale is an extraordinarily earnest book,[1] which only makes the angry, disingenuous reactions against it puzzling this far removed from the controversy. When it was first published in 1951, critics charged Buckley with wanting to institute fascism and theocracy in America's citadels of higher learning. What did he do to provoke such outrage? Paint swastikas on Woodbridge Hall? Take up a collection for a new Inquisition?

Buckley came to Yale in 1946 after a two-year stint as a second lieutenant in the army. He had served in the honor guard for Roosevelt's funeral and ended his career by presiding over about one thousand men who were going through difficult discharges at Fort Sam Houston in San Antonio, Texas. About half the men had contracted venereal diseases, and the other men were awaiting court-martial proceedings. So he looked to Yale as a sort of escape.

Along with his luggage, he said, "I brought with me a firm belief in Christianity and a profound respect for American institutions and traditions." He believed that "free enterprise and limited government had served the country well and would probably continue to do so in the future." And he looked "eagerly to Yale University for allies against secularism and collectivism." He found some takers, but not many.

Buckley had been part of a "small group of students who fought, during the undergraduate days, in the columns of the newspaper [the *Yale Daily News*], in the Political Union, in debates and seminars, against those who seek to subvert religion and individualism." As part of that debate, Buckley had taken the radical position that the alumni of Yale, who fund the school and trade on the prestige of having been educated there, should have some say in what is taught in its classrooms.

After four years of pressing this point, Buckley hadn't made much progress. And so he proposed, with his first book "simply to expose what I regard as an extraordinarily irresponsible educational attitude." Something wrong was being done in the name of "academic freedom" that has "produced one of the most extraordinary incongruities of our time: the institution that derives its moral and financial support from the Christian individualists and then addresses itself to the task of persuading the sons of these supporters to be atheistic socialists."

Buckley had, from the past reactions to his criticisms on campus, "some notion of the bitter opposition that this book will inspire," but he was "through worrying about it," he said, because of his firm conviction that "we are right and they are wrong." Really, his "greatest anguish" was not that his essay would stir the cauldron but that it wouldn't bring it to boil and thereby force real change. The controversy boiled higher than he expected and did produce real change, though it was not quite the kind he hoped for.

The book he produced was a survey of the religious and economic content of undergraduate classes at Yale at mid-century. It was polemical but—according to Buckley—bent over backward to be fair. It documented creeping secularism in the religion and social science and philosophy courses and other academic institutions and student associations. It deplored that creep, along with the tendency of Yale's professors, administrators, and economists to encourage the visible hand of the state to take hold of more of the U.S. economy, to redistribute wealth, and to regulate competition among businesses.

It's true that Buckley got in some zingers, though not many. He ridiculed one popular economic text's incomplete description of the effects of eighteenth-century American commerce by saying, "It is as though a political scientist were to condemn Lincoln as 'That man who put his feet up on the desk and told coarse stories.'"

But for the most part, Buckley earnestly pressed his case that Yale existed to foster interest in certain things, that the alumni and many in the administration actively wanted it to foster said interest, and that they were prohibited from doing so because tenure places most professors out of reach of any administrative attempts to steer them.

Perhaps it was his choice of words that really riled critics up. He didn't just disagree with the current academic trends. He attacked the "superstitions" of academic freedom, as if the pursuits of the administrators and deans of Yale were on the same level as the efforts of witch doctors. Highly trained professionals are likely to take that sort of thing personally.

YALE STRIKES BACK

And take it personally they did. The august *Atlantic Monthly* ran a scathing review in November 1951 by a man with the improbable name McGeorge Bundy, titled "The Attack on Yale."[2]

Bundy was a Yale alum and an employee of the Council on Foreign Relations who would go on to Harvard and the Kennedy and Johnson administrations and Richard Nixon's enemies list. Bundy took umbrage "as a believer in God, a Republican, and a Yale graduate," though clearly not in that order. He called Buckley's effort a "savage attack" and found the book "dishonest in its use of facts, false in its theory, and a discredit to its author." All this by the end of the first paragraph.

Bundy threw every bit of rhetorical tackle in the box at Buckley, from catcalls to condescension to outright smears. He charged that Buckley "holds views of a peculiar and extreme variety, both on economics and on the organization of a university," and had relied on "the flimsiest of evidence or no evidence at all" to support his thesis.

The reviewer deplored the "insidious character of this sort of innuendo and quotation from lectures" because Buckley's liberal use of actual quotes from actual Yale professors from actual lectures that they actually delivered gives the "outsider" no way to "check the context in which the statements were made." And to cover the possibility that his case against the book didn't do it for readers, Bundy also threw in some old-fashioned Catholic baiting for good measure.

Understand, *God and Man at Yale* is not a large-*c* Catholic work. In keeping with his family's mixed religious heritage, Buckley was far more concerned that Christian ideals and practices be bolstered at Yale, even if that would make Yale more Protestant. And, given Yale's history and enrollment, that's very likely what would have happened.

One medium where the book was almost consistently faulted was in the Catholic press. The liberal Catholic lay magazine *Commonweal*, in a bit of overstatement, accused Buckley of advocating "anti-papal economics." Not all Catholic publications were that tough on Buckley, but they recognized there was nothing distinctively Roman about Buckley's call for reform at Yale and didn't cut him any slack.

That didn't matter to Bundy, who tried to use Buckley's religion to hang him. Bundy found it "most remarkable of all" that Buckley would urge "a return to what he considers to be Yale's true religious tradition" without disclosing "he himself is an ardent Roman Catholic." Enter that trademark WASP snobbery: "In view of the pronounced and well-recognized difference between Protestant and Catholic views on education in America, and in view of Yale's Protestant history, it seems strange for any Roman Catholic to undertake to define the Yale religious tradition," Bundy wrote, and "stranger still for Mr. Buckley to venture his prescription with no word or hint to show his"—cue sinister voice, picture hands rubbing together in anticipation—"special allegiance."

The last two words, especially, were an expression not just of contempt but also of straight-out anti-Catholic bigotry. It was that old smear that says Catholics don't think for themselves but substitute blind obedience to Rome, so Protestants don't have to take them seriously. Bundy dismissively wrote that Buckley's "religious orientation, honorable and ancient as it is, emphatically differs from that of Yale," and had thus led Buckley astray.

So Bundy explained things to him. Buckley's "basic argument" Bundy wrote, "is that because the alumni pay the piper, they should call the tune." Wrong, said Bundy. "This argument has no more validity than a proposal that the religious teachings of the Roman Catholic Church should be dictated to the Pope by the Roman Catholic laym[a]n who pays his bills."

MCGEORGE AND THE DRAGON

Buckley said the Yale administration effectively took Bundy's to be the official response. That was putting it too mildly. Bundy closely collaborated with Yale administrators to draft his response to Buckley, and in fact it is likely that they put him up to it and secured its publication in the *Atlantic Monthly*. They ordered thousands of reprints to hand out to alumni as a preemptive way of answering questions, i.e., by not answering questions. Because the review was such an official response, it is interesting now to see some of the odd things that Bundy wrote.

He wrote, for instance, of Buckley's assertion that "Yale has a weak department of religion, a high degree of apathy in the student body, and a number of un-Christian and anti-Christian lecturers in other fields." Even if Buckley were proved right, Bundy penned, "it would not make Yale anti-religious."

But why wouldn't the presence of several anti-Christian lecturers at least open up Yale to legitimate charges of being anti-religious? Because the "weakness of religious teaching has been a national phenomenon for decades, and so has religious apathy among young men." Which answers the question not at all.

Bundy also balked at Buckley's "strict definition of a Christian" that excluded "such men as Jefferson, Emerson, Lincoln, and Yale's own William Howard Taft." It's a bizarre gripe. None of those men were religious scoffers, but they weren't professing Christians.

Then there was the olive branch. Bundy wrote that he "did not wish to say, or seem to say, that Yale is perfect." Nor would he "assert that Christians and conservatives have nothing to worry about at Yale." He granted, "It is possible that Yale should have a stronger and more effective teaching of religion, and that she would benefit from the appointment of a strongly right-wing economist."

These were "fair questions" that the school's "officers must constantly and carefully consider, and anyone who troubles to look will find that these questions get the best attention from the distinguished men who are responsible for the University." It reads like an offer from the administration to campus conservatives: drop this and we'll see what we can do.

Buckley took exception to some of the arguments made against the book, especially the attacks on him using his religion. He insisted that he had not "concealed" anything. It was there for the asking; he just didn't think the fact that he was Catholic had any bearing whatsoever on his calls for religious renewal on a Protestant campus.

Looking back on the experience twenty-five years hence, Buckley said that the "problems raised by *God and Man at Yale* are most definitely with us yet. Some of the predictions made in it have already been realized." He didn't feel that he could really update the book, however, because in order to feel the pulse of a school, you have to have been there recently, and he hadn't. There was one serious attempt made to elect him as an overseer of Yale, but that came up short.

"THEY BURNED THE TEN COMMANDMENTS"

To give readers a picture of Yale today, I went looking and found a mole, a very recent graduate from Yale with a degree in theology. I put the questions to my mole, code-named "Deepthink": What was it like to get a degree in theology from today's Yale? How has the secularization trend that Buckley worried about played out? And how many classes did you have with professing Christians as professors?[3]

Deepthink was full of answers. He, she, or it wrote that of the eight professors under which Deepthink took classes in the religion department, "as far as I know from my own experience and from the religious-studies grapevine, only one would admit his Christianity to his students."

Deepthink told me about the Junior Seminar—whose official title is "Approaches to the Study of Religion"—required of all juniors in the religious studies major. The students studied anthropology at length but "absolutely no theology."

One of the titles on the syllabus was Mary Daly's *Gyn/Ecology: The Metaethics of Radical Feminism*, which Deepthink described as "a deeply stupid book that makes up stories about oppressed medieval witches." Deepthink found this offensive because "every religious studies major has to read it, even though one can get a religious studies degree without ever reading Augustine!"

During "History of the Church to 1200," Deepthink said, "every time we read a patristic text, like Clement of Alexandria or Tertullian or even Augustine, the students would try to come up with secular reasons why these authors wrote what they did."

The students were "apparently unable to take seriously the possibility that early Christians thought women's heads should remain covered, etc., because it's what Christ would have wanted. They found it easier to believe that modesty was always code for patriarchy, apologetics for tribalism, ideas for power. They seemed to think it would be naïve to take these writers at their word."

After three weeks of this, Deepthink became fed up enough to do something obnoxious. As class was breaking up, Deepthink asked, "Just out of curiosity, is anybody here actually, you know, Christian?" The TA very quickly added, "Of course, you don't have to answer. It's none of our business."

Two students answered anyway. "I like the history—I think it's important," said one. "Not really, but I think of this stuff as literature," said the other.

≈

Deepthink also pointed me to a "great horror story from the div school—they burned the Ten Commandments!" *Yale Daily News* reported that on February 21, 2007, "a few dozen students, faculty, administrators and members of the New Haven community gathered in the Divinity School Quadrangle" to celebrate their own version of Ash Wednesday. Call it Protest Ash Wednesday, I guess.

"In lieu of the traditional ashes that are prepared by burning palm leaves, the attendees burned copies of the Ten Commandments and the Bill of Rights and marked each other with the ashes to symbolize the abandonment of the principles set forth by the documents," the *Daily News* reported.[4]

I wasn't able to find another mole to look into the radical activities of the economics majors, so I don't have equivalent stories of them burning greenbacks or stock certificates or calling for luxury taxes on yachts, but it's just possible Buckley was onto something.

BIG CATHOLIC ON CAMPUS

It's become almost a cliché to say that one of the reasons Buckley's charges resonated was that it was a *j'accuse* penned by the very Yaliest of Yalies. With his tall frame, quick wit, piercing eyes, and full, toothsome smile, Buckley quickly won many of his fellow students over to whatever cause he was currently spearheading. One hates to use the phrase "big man on campus," but that's what Buckley definitely ("manifestly," he would say) was.

Buckley had the right pedigree, but he rarely played that up, except insofar as he couldn't help it. He was an excellent debater. He became a member of the university's famous, secret Skull and Bones society (Bundy was also a member, as was George H. W. Bush) and was unanimously elected chairman of the *Yale Daily News*. The school could write off outside critics as people who were disconnected from the life of the university. But with Buckley there wasn't even the excuse that this was a student who was on the fringe of campus activity. He was well liked and right in the thick of it.

In fact, when the Yale administration was looking for

someone to go to the Connecticut legislature to testify against a law that would have forced the university to scrap its religious quotas, including quotas on Catholics, Buckley had obliged them. He had done so because of his belief that private educational institutions should have the right to set their own rules about admissions.

But the line pursued by Yale administrators privately—and through media mouthpieces like Bundy—was that Buckley was an outsider by virtue of his religion, and that he could never be a real Yalie. Therefore his opinions about how Yale should be run were irrelevant. Yale Law School's Professor Fred Rodell wrote in the *Progressive* that he thought even most of Buckley's coreligionists would "resent the un-Christian arrogance of [Buckley's] presentation and, particularly, of his deliberate concealment . . . of his very relevant church affiliation."

Anyone other than Buckley might have called that religious McCarthyism. ("Are you now or have you ever been a member of the Roman Catholic Church, sir? And remember that you are under oath.") Looking back, Buckley simply said that if a reviewer of a book by Rodell on religious freedom had accused the law professor of "deliberate concealment" of the "very relevant" datum that "his name used to be Fred Rodelheim, and his interpretation of the Freedom Clause was tainted in virtue of his lifetime's concealment of his having been born Jewish," then such a charge "would have gone down—quite properly—as anti-Semitism."

Few of Buckley's assailants stopped to consider whether he

was right about Yale's religious tradition. And he most assuredly was. Yale had been founded as a rather strict Congregationalist school. In 1722, Yale's rector, Timothy Cutler—the office of "rector" was later changed to "president"—was fired when he announced his skepticism of Congregationalist orthodoxy and his intention to convert to Anglicanism, though *announced* might be too strong a word. The information appears more likely to have been pried out of him.

According to *Yale: A History*, by Brookes Mather Kelley, on the twelfth of September that year, Cutler "closed the commencement proceedings—one of the colony's great public events of the year—with the customary prayer, but he repeated at the end of it words from the Anglican form: 'and let all the people say, amen.' Consternation! Rumors. Meetings. The next day a dinner was held, and the truth emerged. The rector, several ministers from nearby towns, and the tutor confessed that they either doubted 'the validity of Presbyterian ordination in opposition to Episcopal ordination' or were convinced that presbyterial ordination was invalid."

Consternation! Rumors! Meetings! Presbyterial ordinations! Kelley tried to explain how shocking this revelation was at the time—his book was published in 1974—by saying that "it was something like what might be expected if the current president and faculty of Yale and the leading citizens of several towns around New Haven were all to announce suddenly that some had decided and others were close to deciding that Russian communism was superior to the American economic and political system."[5] Though, actually, by that point, it might not have been so shocking.

Cutler caused quite a stir at the time, but he was far from the last intellectual to be kicked out of Yale over unorthodox beliefs. Buckley was simply reminding liberal Yalies of this historical fact, which they took to be extremely embarrassing. The idea that their predecessors were not as open to whatever tenured profs had to say was seen as something out of the Dark Ages.

SAME STRUGGLE

Sam Tanenhaus, author of a great book on Whittaker Chambers and Bill Buckley's official biographer, said that *God and Man at Yale* contained the seeds of what grew into the conservative movement. It was a brash book that challenged the legitimacy of a venerable American institution, the university, that Buckley charged had been infected by debilitating liberal attitudes. You can hear echoes of this in current conservative criticism of the "MSM" ("mainstream media"—one of the world's most annoying abbreviations) and other institutions—from churches to charities.

It's an annoyingly effective criticism, if for no other reason than that it's often true. Institutions over time do tend to be run by people whose politics and attitudes are more liberal than their predecessors, and they tend to prefer people with similar pedigrees in new hires. The result, absent any serious effort to retrench, is a slow, steady leftward drift. Buckley's broadside lent conservative skepticism of American institutions an intellectual respectability that it had not previously enjoyed.

Those institutions didn't, and don't, like the criticism. In the blowback against the book, we caught a glimpse of the polarization that would later slowly grip the country: Conservatives question why liberals should run the show; liberals respond by questioning the conservative's motives; people choose sides; anathemas are hurled. Over time, conservatives would be virtually excluded from teaching positions in most colleges, in part because the academic community came to view them as a threat. Best not to take chances that one of them would turn into the next William F. Buckley.

God and Man at Yale also laid out the blueprint for the postwar conservative movement. In one of the most praised and attacked passages of the book, Buckley declared, "I believe that the struggle between Christianity and atheism is the most important in the world. I further believe that the struggle between individualism and collectivism is the same struggle reproduced on another level."

Buckley later admitted that he didn't write those sentences. A Yale philosophy professor and close Buckley confidante had proposed them. Buckley wrote that when he "saw the suggested formulation, written out on the margin of my manuscript in Willmore Kendall's bold green script," he had "suspected they would cause difficulty," and he paused to consider that, "but there was a nice rhetorical resonance and an intrinsic, almost nonchalant suggestion of an exciting symbiosis, so I let it pass."

The young controversialist had the right intuition. He knew that there was something in those sentences that promised to be revolutionary, but he didn't fully realize what he had at the time. In his public defense of the book, he reflected simply that he "did not renounce" those words because it would have proved embarrassing, because of his "loyalty to my mentor," Kendall, and because "I was tickled by the audacity" of it and "not unamused by the sputtering outrage of its critics."

What he didn't know then was that audacity is the stuff political movements are made of.

3

MERCURIAL YEARS

After his graduation from Yale, Bill Buckley worked, briefly, for the CIA. His professor, Willmore Kendall, had been part of the Office of Strategic Services (OSS) during World War II. The OSS became the CIA in the postwar years as the American government readied itself for the long struggle against the Soviet Union. The CIA wanted recruiters at America's top universities, and Kendall was happy to steer some of the best and brightest toward America's intelligence services.

The sales pitch worked in this case because the Korean War broke out, threatening to remobilize Army Second Lieutenant Buckley. Kendall approached his student about joining instead what CIA agents then called "the company," and Buckley decided to give it a go, if the CIA would have him.

Buckley deferred grad school and stayed on at Yale to teach Spanish, his first language, to underclassmen. The CIA wanted

Buckley as a deep-cover agent, not an analyst. It was while he was undergoing evaluation by the CIA and teaching at the university that Buckley wrote *God and Man at Yale*. It was during this same period that Buckley married Patricia "Pat" Taylor, from the wealthy Taylor clan of Vancouver, British Columbia.

Pat was Anglican by birth and occasional observance and would not convert to marry Bill, but she did consent to having any Buckley children raised Catholic. They tied the knot in the summer of 1950 in a large wedding conducted by the Catholic archbishop of Vancouver and later blessed at the Taylor residence by an Anglican divine.

Buckley was trained in spycraft in Washington DC and then sent by the CIA to Mexico City under his own name. The cover was that he was poking around Mexico to see about some of his old man's business interests. Mexico City at the time was a hotbed of international intrigue. It was where Joseph Stalin dispatched an assassin to pickax the exiled Russian revolutionary leader Leon Trotsky to death, for instance. The dying Trotsky kept his bodyguards from killing the assassin so as to expose the plot and exact retribution posthumously.

Decades later Buckley would bump into Miguel Alemán Valdés, president of Mexico's leftist Institutional Revolutionary Party (PRI) during Buckley's CIA sojourn in Mexico. They were both skiing in Switzerland when Valdés asked Buckley what he had been up to in Mexico. "I tried to undermine your regime, Mr. President," Buckley replied.[1]

But really Buckley's experience there had been mostly dull.

His training had been extensive, but he didn't have the chance to use it much. He spent most of the time encouraging anti-Communists to run for leadership in Mexican student organizations and editing a book by Eudocio Ravines, a Peruvian former Communist, about Communist designs for world domination.

Buckley's boss in Mexico was Howard Hunt, a CIA man on the way up, whose name will no doubt be familiar, if not infamous, to many readers, but we'll get there in a few chapters. Hunt was impressed with Buckley. In fact, the two got along so well that Buckley later became godfather to three of Hunt's children. Normally the title godfather is honorific in that it doesn't mean a great deal (Marlon Brando's star turn notwithstanding), but in this case Buckley's honorific would give him early insight into one of American politics' great tragedies.

Mexico City wasn't all bad for the Buckleys. Bill enjoyed meeting some of his dad's old associates and would go back there several times. But Pat suffered a tubal pregnancy while there, and it also became more and more obvious that Bill's talents could be put to better use back in America. Even so, they might have stuck it out for more than the nine months that they lasted there. The thing that finally forced their hand was the *New York Times* best-seller list.

God and Man at Yale was, in the jargon of journalism, "written on spec." *Spec* is short for *speculation*. Nothing was guaranteed in advance because Buckley did not have a contract when he undertook to write the book. He researched and wrote it and sent it to the upstart conservative publisher Henry Regnery, founder of the firm that bears his name. Regnery promptly accepted it and published the book while Bill was in Mexico City.

It sold better than expected. Far better. Will Buckley loaned Regnery money to promote the book, which helped. But the hostile reviews made people, especially students, want to see what all the fuss was about. It climbed the charts.

It was not feasible for Bill to stay a deep-cover agent in Mexico while his name was being splashed all over American newspapers. So he quit the CIA to come back to the United States and enter the contest of ideas, full-time. But how to do that?

FUNNY THINGS

The early 1950s were, for Bill and Pat Buckley, a time of frustration and flux. Bill thought many of the reviews were so outlandish because there were so many more liberal journals of opinion than nonliberal ones. The reviewers felt they could get away with it, and that had major echo chamber effects.

There were a few nonliberal magazines, true. There was the *Freeman* in Chicago and the *American Mercury* in New York and the weekly newspaper *Human Events* in the nation's capital and very few other voices, save *Reader's Digest* and the scattered editorial pages of newspapers that were slowly but surely becoming more liberal. It was in these forums that Buckley's best seller got its best treatment. It was reviewed favorably in the *Freeman* and the *American Mercury*. Both offered him jobs.

He took the assistant editor job at the *American Mercury*.

The magazine had been founded in the 1920s by H. L. Mencken and had featured the writing of some of America's notable writers, from Ernest Hemingway to Theodore Dreiser. It had gone through tumult. A few offensive articles led to major fights with local censors and with the U.S. Post Office, and the magazine changed hands regularly. The acquisitions led to several editorial turnovers, which changed the nature of the magazine. ⋅

When Bill came on in 1952, it was a more explicitly right-wing magazine than it had been, and that political turn would eventually prove its undoing, as it drifted into the "fever swamps" of genuine neo-Nazism. Bill worked there only a few months and left over the fact that one of its articles had been spiked—that is, not published because of editorial caprice.

That experience soured Bill on the idea of working for somebody else. The *Freeman* repeated its offer to hire him, but he turned it down, and that only saved him from further frustration. The conservative senator Robert Taft of Ohio, who had twice tried and twice failed to capture the Republican nomination, looked as if he would finally pull it off until former Supreme Allied Commander and five-star general Dwight Eisenhower threw his hat into the ring.

The *Freeman* was controlled by an editorial board that was deeply divided over who to endorse, and the fighting between the Taft men and the I-Like-Ikers tore the magazine apart as the two candidates battled it out all the way to the Republican convention in Chicago. As a man firmly in the Taft camp, Buckley wouldn't have lasted long.

In 1952 and '53, the Buckleys and the lumpen mass of conservative voters in the country experienced parallel euphorias—and disappointments.

In November, Eisenhower destroyed his opponent, Illinois governor Adlai Stevenson, leading to Stevenson's most memorable quip, from his concession speech, "A funny thing happened on the way to the White House . . ." Eisenhower won thirty-nine states for an Electoral College victory of 442 to 89, and the Republicans picked up two Senate seats and twenty-two House seats, giving them narrow control of Congress. As Senate majority leader, Taft would enjoy some considerable influence in the Eisenhower administration; but he died of cancer on July 31, 1953, and the administration took a definite left turn after that.

On September 28, Pat delivered a son, Christopher Taylor Buckley. The next May she suffered another tubal pregnancy, reducing her already considerably lowered chances of conception to zero. The Buckleys had wanted a large family, but "providence," Bill said, had other ideas. It didn't immediately inform them what it had up its sleeve.

PIXIE DUST-UP

After the success of *God and Man at Yale* and the failure of Bill's attempt to keep a regular magazine journalism job, a lot was up in the air. Henry Regnery suggested that Bill write a book on conservative philosophy, but that's not what moved the young best-selling polemicist.

Instead Buckley proposed his one and only cowritten book, with Yale debate partner and brother-in-law L. Brent Bozell Jr. (The Brent Bozell who founded Media Research Center and appears regularly on television is his son.) It would be about the controversies surrounding the man of the moment, the communist-hunting Wisconsin senator Joseph McCarthy.

Regnery signed off on it, but the project that eventually became *McCarthy and His Enemies* was plagued with problems. The writing took longer and was lengthier than expected. The cover price was $6.50—far higher than the industry standard for popular books at the time. Buckley and Bozell didn't always see eye-to-eye on why they were writing the book or what exactly they were calling for, and they fought about it.

Bozell wanted to use McCarthyism to effectively outlaw certain viewpoints. Buckley thought they should focus all their legal fire on people who knowingly worked for or cooperated with the Soviet Union and Soviet front groups and use a mix of argument and ostracism to deal with innocent fellow travelers. Their disagreement about tactics—how much was too much?—would fissure into a broken friendship later in life.

Worse, they made the disastrous decision to try to get Senator McCarthy himself to endorse the book. He refused, citing all the parts in the book that questioned his decisions or faulted his judgment or command of the facts. Buckley and Bozell attempted to water down the offending passages to get the senator's approval, but all that did was make the book seem less objective. Yes, McCarthy still declined to endorse a book that defended him from most attacks.

The volume finally appeared in 1954, one month before the infamous Army-McCarthy hearings that led to McCarthy's censure, downfall, and early death from recklessness fed by excess drink.

NO TO JOE

But McCarthy*ism* was another matter. From the outset, the purpose of *McCarthy and His Enemies* had been to vindicate the movement that the Wisconsin senator represented and only secondarily the man himself. Among committed anti-Communists, there was a running, lively, and largely private debate about the wisdom of backing McCarthy.

Henry Regnery sent an advance copy of the Buckley/Bozell book to Whittaker Chambers, the American who had been a Soviet agent before he "flipped" and put former high-ranking U.S. State Department official and prominent think-tank denizen Alger Hiss in jail. Regnery asked if Chambers thought the book was fair to McCarthy and the anti-Communist cause in general. Chambers said it was a great book and a fine and measured defense of McCarthyism, but he cautioned that there remained the problem of the man himself.

To be sure, Chambers told Regnery the book stated McCarthy's case "with understanding, clarity, cogency, good humor, knowingness and more generosity than many would be willing to indulge simply on the face of some of the cited facts." He called it "readable from start to end."

But Chambers declined to endorse the book because, as he wrote in a February 7, 2004, letter to Bill Buckley—the first direct contact between the two men—he was terrified the senator "will one day make some irreparable blunder which will play directly into the hands of our common enemy and discredit the whole anti-Communist effort for a long while to come."[2]

Richard Nixon, who had put the Hiss-Chambers case in the limelight, also thought that McCarthy was dangerous and unpredictable and therefore bad for anti-Communism. He would later tell research assistant Jeffrey Hart about the time he saved hated gossip columnist Drew Pearson's life—from McCarthy's assault. The story is recounted in Hart's book on America in the '50s, *When the Going Was Good*.

"I was having dinner at the Sulgrave Club in Washington," Nixon told Hart over martinis in his Manhattan town house, in the 1960s, "and when I went down to the coatroom, I saw Joe McCarthy in there with his hands around Pearson's throat. He was strangling him, also trying to knee him in the groin. McCarthy was a big bear of a man—he'd been a boxer—and Pearson was beginning to turn grey."

When McCarthy saw Nixon, he "gave Pearson a terrific slap on the face with one hand and said 'That's one for you, Dick!' " Nixon then "grabbed [McCarthy] by the arm, and tried to pull him off Pearson" and attempted a small joke to defuse things, "something about letting a Quaker make peace here."

"He's . . . evil," McCarthy shot back, and while the two were discussing the finer points of Pearson's character, the columnist "scurried out of the coatroom and got away." "It was pretty close," Nixon said.[3]

Buckley and Bozell wrote that "as long as McCarthyism fixes its goal with its present precision, it is a movement around which men of good will and stern morality can close ranks."[4] *Not so fast*, said Mark Royden Winchell. By voting to formally condemn McCarthy on December 2, 1964, he argued "the men of good will and stern morality who constituted the United States Senate (some of whom were conservative Republicans) finally closed ranks to censure the *imprecision* of McCarthyism."[5]

TOO MUCH DECENCY

Buckley and Bozell took on a nearly impossible task in their attempt to mount a limited defense of Senator McCarthy and a more robust defense of the movement that he represented. The case for McCarthy was never that he was perfect, or even always prudent, but that he was onto something important and that his accusations didn't amount to a "witch hunt." Witches, by and large, aren't real. The problem of Communist infiltration in the U.S. government was very real, they argued, and should be dealt with publicly.

It's hard to argue that they were wrong on the first point. The U.S. government first successfully tested nuclear weapons technology during July 1945. The Soviet Union was far behind, but thanks to spies and informants, including Ethel and Julius Rosenberg, Harry Gold, David Greenglass, Theodore Hall, Allan May, and Klaus Fuchs, it had its first successful nuclear test in August 1949. The Russians were helped along by detailed schematics, theoretical spadework, reports of U.S tests, and even reports on the amount of fissile material that the United States was refining every year, and thus how many nuclear weapons America could have on hand.

Anti-Communist but non-McCarthyite Democrats, such as Harry Truman, knew that there was a problem of Soviet infiltration of the U.S. government but tried to deal with it quietly. Alger Hiss had been a prominent representative of the State Department to the Yalta Conference in 1945. When it was learned that he was a Soviet spy, the Truman administration pushed him out of the government to the Carnegie Endowment for International Peace, where, it was hoped, he couldn't do much damage. The wise men at State thought that was the decent and expedient thing to do. McCarthyites and a jury thought otherwise.

McCarthyites argued that it was possible to be too clever and too subtle and too decent about such things. They believed the threat posed by Communism went beyond the usual considerations of international politics, and they were often enraged when the understandable concerns that liberals had for civil liberties were inflated to the point that McCarthyites—people who wanted to get serious about the current threat—were treated as the enemy.

Eleanor Roosevelt, for example, wrote a column likening McCarthyism to Hitlerism. In *Up from Liberalism*, Buckley recounted how he said on television that meant that if she ran into McCarthy and Andrei Vishinsky, head of the Soviet delegation to the United Nations, at a party, she would probably, in fairness, refuse to shake both men's hands.

A reporter asked her about that, and Roosevelt "answered emphatically that she would shake hands with both Vishinsky *and* McCarthy" and, in fact, she said that "she once *had* shaken McCarthy's hand." This led to the obvious question, put to her by readers of *Woman's Home Companion* magazine, "Would you also have felt that it was right to shake hands with Hitler?" Well, she answered, "In Adolf Hitler's early days I might have considered it, but after he had begun his mass killings, I don't think I could have borne it."

Buckley then cheekily suggested, "Mrs. Roosevelt's philosophy of hand-shaking doesn't emerge from the data." The logical syllogism, he said, would look something like this:

> **Proposition A:** E. R. will not shake hands with those who are guilty of mass killings.
> **Proposition B:** E. R. will shake hands with Andrei Vishinsky.
> **Conclusion:** Andrei Vishinsky is not guilty of mass killings.

The only problem with that conclusion, he pointed out, was that it was directly contradicted by the ugly history that a special

U.S. government commission—empaneled by Roosevelt's husband's own administration—had revealed, which "settled forever Vishinsky's blood guilt."

Vishinsky wasn't just some harmless, middling bureaucrat. He had served as the chief prosecutor at Joseph Stalin's murderous purge show trials. Yet that didn't stop Roosevelt from shaking his hand or working with him on the United Nations' declaration of human rights. Buckley offered up a "comparable activity" for our consideration. How about "chatting with [Joseph] Goebbels about a genocide agreement"?[6]

WHY NOT BUCKLEY?

Buckley later reflected, when he was promoting his novel *The Redhunter*, on how much McCarthy had done to cause his own undoing. McCarthy was impulsive, drunken, violent, and possibly a morphine addict. He was condemned by colleagues and died an early death in 1957. But Buckley couldn't shake the conviction that McCarthy's cause was essentially right and just.

Where did his certainty come from? At a conference in the summer of 2009 put on by the Portsmouth Institute about the religious side of Bill Buckley, several participants argued that it was his religion. Clark Judge said Buckley saw that the "Cold war was not just about strategic tensions, a standoff with another nuclear power. . . . [He] argued that Cold War was at its root a moral struggle—about the nature of man and society, of freedom, and of free will."[7]

"We have heard at this conference McGeorge Bundy's odious putdown of [*God and Man at Yale*]—a not-so-veiled anti-Catholic sneer," said Judge. "But one thing Bundy got right was that Bill's understanding of the Communist challenge was informed of his Catholicism, reflecting a quality of moral insight almost entirely lost on the Protestant establishment of the day."

That may be going a bit far. There were plenty of staunch Protestant anti-Communists in the 1950s. The revivalist Reverend Billy Graham was very much invested in the struggle against Communism. Screen Actors Guild president Ronald Reagan, raised in a fundamentalist Disciples of Christ congregation, was struggling against reds and naming names before Buckley graduated from Yale. Nixon and Chambers were Quakers.

But it is true that Catholics felt especially invested in the struggle against Communism. Rome viewed Moscow as the champion of a rival, false, malevolent creed. From places such as Mexico, the Church had all the evidence it needed of what happens when aggressive collectivists and secularists take over. Masses featured prayers for the conversion of Russia. Most American Catholic politicians—from John F. Kennedy to Eugene McCarthy to Tailgunner Joe himself—were staunch anti-Communists.

It's *possible* to lean too hard on Buckley's religion as an explanation for why he argued "X" or did "Y." But Communism, his father's awful experience in Mexico, his religion, and his experience all lined up in the same direction. The Buckleys had been isolationists until Pearl Harbor, but with the war over, they decided that the threat of expansionist Communism posed by the Soviet Union was great enough to justify a massive military buildup, serious cloak-and-dagger initiatives, and, of course, a public campaign to fight Communist infiltration of the U.S. government and collectivist trends generally.

With Senator McCarthy sidelined, that campaign needed better promotion and another standard-bearer. Preferably, the man would be adept at argument, a risk taker and trailblazer who was capable of taking on this new medium of television.

4

HOTTEST THING
IN TOWN

Our subject is Bill Buckley, not *National Review*, but it's fun to consider the crazy cast of characters who worked for the magazine early on. They influenced Buckley greatly and often infuriated him. Here are only a few of them:

Whittaker Chambers: The former Communist spy and literary editor of *Time* magazine, who wrote *Witness*, the biggest anti-Communist blockbuster of all time, and translated *Bambi* into English. Chambers was a pessimist, if not a depressive, whose politics were eclectic. He called himself a "man of the right" but never a conservative. He was a Quaker, a farmer, and an extraordinarily talented writer. He was an extremely reluctant contributor to *National Review*.

Brent Bozell: Buckley's Yale debate partner—tall, with red hair and prominent ears that stuck out. He was a fierce orator and a skilled polemicist who would pen and then disavow one of the classic texts of American conservatism. Bozell was a Catholic convert who married Bill's sister Trish. He naturally gravitated toward extremes, helped along by his bipolar disorder.

James Burnham: Not so much the voice of moderation at *National Review* as the voice of moderate Republicanism. The author of *The Managerial Revolution* and *The Machiavellians* was a former CIA hand, and the de facto executive editor of the magazine for many years. He pushed *National Review* to embrace mainstream politicians, including Eisenhower and Rockefeller, and was a staunch Cold Warrior.

Garry Wills: A former Jesuit seminarian who was constantly reinventing himself, but doing so with the prose of an angel. By the time he wrote *Confessions of a Conservative*, the title was not very accurate. Wills started out as a Cold Warrior and something of a European-style conservative who was influenced by the economic theories and religious thought of G. K. Chesterton and Hillaire Belloc. He ended up endorsing just about any old liberal position that you could think of.

Frank Meyer: The former Communist who feuded with several prominent conservative figures, though not violently. Meyer was a philosopher by training who policed the magazine's review section for ideological deviations, a night owl, and a Jew who converted to Catholicism before his death in 1972.

Willmore Kendall: Buckley's former Yale prof and CIA recruiter, who was an absolute expert at feuding with people.

He infuriated the administration at Yale so much that they bought out his tenure. Kendall was a Catholic convert and a bit of a scoundrel. He once traveled to the Vatican to have not one but two marriages annulled.

William Rusher: The tireless promoter, publisher, and conservative activist. Rusher always had a new scheme up his sleeves. He at one point tried to talk Ronald Reagan into running for president on a third-party ticket.

FOUNDING FOUR

There are four things you probably should know about the founding of *National Review*. The first is that Bill Buckley wanted a magazine, but he didn't want to start one from scratch. He made offers to take over the *Freeman* and *Human Events* and was rebuffed by the owners and directors. He also, incredibly, attempted to buy the liberal Catholic magazine *Commonweal*. Imagine how different history would have been if that had gone through.

The second thing to know is that the founding of *National Review* (in 1955) only made sense as part of a larger and much more ambitious project. Before Buckley, America had been a country with diverse strains of free-market liberal, anti-Communist, and traditionalist thinking. Through *National Review*, Buckley sought to gather those all under the sail of "conservatism" and fix the newly cast conservative cannons on the enemies of collectivism, liberalism, and Communism, but he didn't have any illusions that such a thing could be accomplished without other parallel institutions that did not yet exist.

National Review was thus one of only several foundings in which Bill Buckley played a vital part. He also helped to start the conservative youth organization Young Americans for Freedom in 1960. The first meeting was held at his parents' estate in Sharon, Connecticut, and the organization's charter document, the so-called Sharon statement, bears the indelible stamp of Buckley's politics and personality. The young individualists got together to hash out a statement, and they came up with one that was traditionalist, laissez-faire, and stoutly anti-Communist. Who could have seen *that* coming?

It was easy for Buckley to exercise outsized influence over young right-wingers because, as historian Lee Edwards noted, they adored him: "We young conservatives expressed our awe and love for Bill by emulating him—we raised our eyebrows, we drawled, we searched our Thesaurus for the rare and the obscure, we strove to be outrageous."[1] Though few ever quite managed to outrage as effectively as Buckley.

Then there was the Conservative Party of New York. Buckley and a group of Republicans who were disgusted with the tilt of their own state party established a real alternative for voters. They stole the idea from the Left. Thanks to New York's quirky ballot laws, where a candidate may run on more than one party line, small parties that provide the crucial margin of victory for a candidate can enjoy huge influence.

New York's Liberal Party mustered huge influence, and state Republicans were dominated by such liberal Republican heavyweights as Nelson Rockefeller, Jacob Javits, and John Lindsay. That left New York conservatives with little choice other than the fourth-party route if they wanted to have any influence on the state's politics. Buckley encouraged them to take the plunge.

Third, the magazine served as a springboard for Buckley's countless public campaigns, and helped to catapult him onto other things, as we'll soon see.

The fourth thing to know is that *National Review* in the early years—and I say this descriptively, not judgmentally, and Buckley shares some of the blame for this—is that it was not much like the *National Review* of today.

ATHWART HISTORY

True, certain conventions are still observed in the modern *National Review* that go back to its founding. It still has the same blue frame on every cover, an idea stolen from *Time* magazine and tweaked. It still has a large, quite good, unsigned editorial section in the front of every issue. And it is still broadly concerned with issues of conservative orthodoxy. But it does not have the same spirited independence that the early *National Review* enjoyed.

Now: It would be hard to imagine *National Review* not endorsing the Republican candidate for president. George W.

Bush got the magazine's guarded and then enthusiastic endorsements, and a big pat on the back on the way out. John McCain, who had been a thorn in the side of movement conservatives and almost switched parties, also got the thumbs-up.

Then: *National Review* declined to formally endorse Eisenhower in 1956 and again withheld its endorsement from Richard Nixon in the 1960 election. In fact, the sort of moderate "modern Republicanism" that Ike and Nixon represented was the target of much ridicule by Buckley and company. The kids today might call them hard-core.

This is not always well understood by people who work at *National Review*. In 2005, America's Future Foundation put on a debate about the future of conservatism. Nick Gillespie, then editor of the libertarian magazine *Reason*, tried to paint conservatives as a bunch of cavemen. He scoffed that *National Review* announced that its mission would be to "stand athwart history, yelling stop!" and asked the audience how you get more retrograde than that.

His take really missed the mark. It was really history with a capital *H* that *National Review* had objected to. At the time of the magazine's founding, Leftists and Communists would regularly claim that the forces of history were bringing about a new Marxian reality.

In John le Carré's 1963 novel, *The Spy Who Came in from the Cold*, the hero realizes that he's in love with someone from the other side when she tells him she believes not in religion but in unstoppable historical forces:

Q: [*Upon learning that she doesn't believe in God*]
   "Then what do you believe in?"
A: "History."
Q: "Oh, Liz . . . oh no. You're not a bloody
   Communist?"[2]

What the editors of *National Review* were saying was that history, small *h*, was not on the side of the Communists—and they were right about that.

When a young reporter wrote up the event on *National Review*'s Web site, no mention was made of this monstrous misrepresentation of the magazine's past. Instead, the reporter gushed that Gillespie "certainly surpassed the Pabst Blue Ribbon swilling, Death Cab for Cutie loving, hipster circa 2001 image I had going in."[3]

Buckley would call that "invincible ignorance," if he was in a mood to be generous.

YELLING, "STOP!"

Buckley would say that, yes, he had helped to midwife the conservative movement but that if he hadn't done it, somebody else would have. Perhaps. Yet the first editorial of his magazine made something like the polar-opposite claim. "Let's face it," wrote the editors, ". . . it seems altogether possible that did *National Review* not exist, no one would have invented it."[4]

That was because the magazine and the movement that it hoped to represent "stands athwart history, yelling Stop, at a time when no one is inclined to do so, or to have much patience with those who so urge it." By no one, they meant American society's elites. They explained that "literate America [had] rejected conservatism in favor of radical social experimentation." Literate America had therefore rejected the principles "so clearly enunciated in the enabling documents of our Republic." The opening shot gave a good flavor of things to come:

National Review Editorial	My Translation
"The launching of a conservative weekly journal of opinion in a country widely assumed to be a bastion of conservatism at first glance looks . . . [rather] like publishing a royalist weekly within the walls of Buckingham Palace."	America is a conservative country.
"We feel gentlemanly doubts when asserting the superiority of capitalism to socialism, of republicanism to centralism . . . of anything to anything."	Relativism is bad.
"I happen to prefer champagne to ditchwater," said the benign old wrecker of the ordered society, Oliver Wendell Holmes, "but there is no reason to suppose that the cosmos does."	It is caused, ultimately, by atheism.

"One must recently have lived on or close to a college campus to have a vivid intimation of what has happened."	Liberals run academia.
"Since ideas rule the world, the ideologues, having won over the intellectual class, simply walked in and started to run things."	Liberals run the country.
"There never was an age of conformity quite like this one, or a camaraderie quite like the Liberals'."	Liberals are narrow-minded.
"We are non-licensed nonconformists."	Conservatives are the real liberals.
"This is dangerous business in a Liberal world, as every editor of this magazine can readily show by pointing to his scars."	Conservatives are persecuted by liberals.
"Conservatives in this country—at least those who have not made their peace with the New Deal, and there is serious question whether there are others . . ."	True conservatives are radicals.
"The well-fed Right['s] . . . ignorance and amorality have never been exaggerated for the same reason that one cannot exaggerate infinity."	Nonradical so-called conservatives are wicked.

"A vigorous and incorruptible journal of conservative opinion is—dare we say it?—as necessary to better living as Chemistry."	Conservatives needed to join the battle of ideas and—lo!—a wandering knight offered up his services.

The editors also included the prospectus that had been sent to investors of the magazine. It declared that the domestic growth of government "must be fought relentlessly," endorsed an "organic moral order," and came out swinging against "Social Engineers," "intellectual cliques," "bipartisanship," "union monopolies," and "world government." Communism, said *National Review*, was "the [twentieth] century's most blatant force of Satanic utopianism." And "coexistence" was judged "neither desirable nor possible nor honorable; we find ourselves irrevocably at war with communism and shall oppose any substitute for victory."

The opening statement was a collective expression of the editors. It stressed the shared struggle not only of the "two men and one woman" who produced the first issue but also the "score of professional writers" who had pitched in and helped out. And it thanked the "more than one hundred and twenty investors [who] made this magazine possible," including "over fifty men and women of small means [who] invested less than one thousand dollars apiece in it."

That was all well and good, but the principal investor was

Bill Buckley. His father put up $100,000 in 1955 dollars to help get *National Review* off the ground, and Bill owned all the voting shares in the corporation. He made many of the edits and all the final calls for what went into the magazine. He was, in effect, a dictator, though a mostly benign one.

I mention that because the final lines of the statement of principals are vintage Buckley, especially the final flourish. *National Review* said that it offered "a position that has not grown old under the weight of a gigantic, parasitic bureaucracy, a position untempered by the doctoral dissertations of a generation of Ph.Ds in social architecture, unattenuated by a thousand vulgar promises to a thousand different pressure groups, uncorroded by a cynical contempt for human freedom. And that, ladies and gentlemen, leaves us just about the hottest thing in town."

BACK IN THE USSR

National Review's most famous anti-Communist crusades probably occurred in 1959 and 1960. The Eisenhower administration invited Soviet premier Nikita Khrushchev to tour the United States, and the editors thought that the invite "to spend thirteen days in America, including a visit to Hollywood, conveyed . . . a kind of conviviality at odds with a correct U.S. perspective on the Communist enterprise."[5]

They did everything they could to register a protest. After the first visit, the *National Review* editors took some solace in the fact that Eisenhower wasn't smiling in any of the official photos. Maybe Ike was trying to convey a message, or maybe he was just annoyed with all the trouble they'd created for him.

Khrushchev came back to the United States the next year. He was scheduled to land by boat, in *National Review*'s own backyard in Manhattan, New York, to attend a meeting of the United Nations, and then wind through the country again—to Washington DC. One of the editors suggested they find a way to dye the East River, where the Russians would dock, bright red.

Buckley didn't dismiss this idea and in fact suggested, from his considerable nautical experience, that they use the dye marker that small boats use to broadcast distress on ocean currents. "My thought," he wrote, "was to empty a quart of dye marker into the East River from the 59 Street Bridge, which would serve to redden a few acres through which the *Baltika* would need to plow to reach its designated quay on the east side of Manhattan."

The elements had other ideas. Buckley, "after consulting the tide tables [he] kept in [his] sailboat," discovered that the current was all wrong. From the bridge on that September day, they would redden not the Communists but Connecticut. So they conceived an airstrike instead. Buckley decided to rent a plane to fly a banner reading, "KHRUSHCHEV IS A LIAR." But the Federal Aviation Agency was way ahead of them: it had issued an order "prohibiting private flights over Manhattan between the hours of 8 A.M. and 12 noon on the critical day."

Undaunted, they rented out Carnegie Hall and sold it out.

The audience thrilled to the anti-Communist rhetoric. Buckley was angry, and it showed in his address.[6] He denounced just about the entire American foreign policy establishment, including Richard Nixon. ("If you have to throw something at Khrushchev," Nixon had said, "throw flowers.")

That the Russian leader should receive such an enthusiastic diplomatic response recognition—"not four years after shocking history itself by the brutalities of Budapest," months after the recent dust-up of the downed American U-2 spy plane in Degtyarsk (in Russia's Ural region), weeks since the premier "last shrieked his intention of demolishing the West," and mere days since Khrushchev had told an American magazine that Russia intended to rule all of Berlin, Buckley warned—"will teach him something about the West that some of us wish he might never have known."

But Buckley told the crowd not to despair, because "in the West there lie, however encysted, the ultimate resources, which are moral in nature." The Soviet leader, he said, "is *not* aware that the gates of hell shall not prevail against us." And: "In the end we will bury *him*."

5

A TIME FOR LOSING

"Fusionism" sounds like something that would be more at home in the hard sciences than in political science. It's the term used to describe how Bill Buckley managed to make modern conservatism both intellectually palatable and politically salable.

It was not too much of a stretch in the 1950s and '60s to convince religious and nonreligious Americans that Communism, at least as it was practiced in the USSR and its puppet regimes, was evil. Full stop. The show trials and gulags and forced famines were pretty good evidence that something was rotten in Russia. Many Christians argued this evil had religious roots.

In the preface to his best-selling 1952 autobiography, *Witness*, former Soviet spy Whittaker Chambers traced Communism back to the garden of Eden—the part where the serpent tempted Eve to go ahead and eat that forbidden fruit, "and ye shall be as gods."[1] According to this interpretation, the fatal flaw of

Communism was that it tried to replace God with Big Brother. However, it *was* a stretch to then say that because Communism was evil, so was the modern welfare state. People could see a clear difference between the two. One was murderous; the other could be a bother and a nuisance, but it delivered provisions and services to people who might otherwise go without.

Buckley wanted a conservatism that treated progressivism or liberalism only somewhat less contemptuously than it did Communism. He thought that, granted, Communism is worse, but the logic of Leftist thought pulled in the same wrong direction and could produce similar horrifying outcomes.

Recall in *God and Man at Yale* where Buckley proposed the struggle between collectivism and individualism was essentially the same struggle as the fight between godless Communism and what was left of Western civilization. It was a hard sell. McCarthyism made it easier to make the case. People were more likely to take you seriously when you claimed that the progressive program posed a threat to the good of society when conservatives could show that FDR's and Truman's very progressive administrations were riddled with actual Communists and also show academia to be chock-a-block with reds and fellow travelers.

In debate with prominent liberals, Buckley often shocked them by bringing up their more unsavory associations. He had rejected the notion that the conservatives should use McCarthyism to, in effect, outlaw liberalism, but that was as charitable as he was willing to be. He fully intended to sow doubt and create division by being rude enough to engage in a little guilt by Communism.

Casting doubt on liberals was a great way of casting doubt on the goodness of their plans and programs.

That tactic was not very effective against certain targets, obviously. When Robert Welch, former candy producer and founder of the John Birch Society, accused Eisenhower of being a "dedicated, conscious agent of the Communist conspiracy," historian Russell Kirk said dismissively, "Eisenhower is not a Communist. He's a golfer!"[2]

There was a further problem with using McCarthyism to get around the suspicion that Buckley was reaching too far. It wasn't just liberals that Buckley had to contend with. As with the controversy over his first book, he found that potential allies objected to his love—and, no, *love* isn't too strong a word for it—for capitalism. What's more, his enthusiasm initially ran into all kinds of opposition *among conservatives*.

There is a strain of right-wing European thought that is both antiliberal and antimarket, which makes sense when you consider that liberalism started out as a pro-market philosophy. Kirk, the Michigan Tory who tried to trace the roots of an American conservative tradition, thought that markets were important but that Buckley was taking things a bit far. Chambers was constantly pressing the point with Buckley that capitalism was hostile to tradition and thus the enemy of true conservatism.

George Scialabba—in his 2009 collection *What Are Intellectuals Good For?*—pointed to a preface that Buckley wrote for an essay about European individualism. Buckley called "the discovery of the individual" the "preeminent fact of modern

European history" and added that conservatism is "the politics of the individual."

Scialabba, whose politics are progressive, was flabbergasted by that claim. "Buckley's fervent and wholly orthodox Catholicism is his deepest commitment, his essential identity, as he has often made clear," Scialabba wrote. "Did he really not understand that [the prefaced essay] is describing the decline of religious orthodoxy as a precondition for the emergence of individuality?" Could Buckley not see that "individualism and secularism are inseparable"?[3]

Now, there are serious problems with Scialabba's challenge. It misses some important wrinkles in Buckley's religious thinking, and it leans on the rickety theory that as nations become richer, their citizens automatically shrug off religious observance. That isn't always so. America, for instance, manages to be a very rich, very individualistic nation, with high rates of religious observance—at least as measured against European nations.

But the feeling that markets undermine morals was powerful, and Buckley had to take it seriously. It is telling that he reached not for an economic argument but for a moral one. His response began with a question: "What is virtue?"

FREE TO CHOOSE

Which brings us back to that *faux* sci-fi term *fusionism*. The idea was so-called because it promised to provide a way to fuse competing but related ideologies. It was the brainchild of

National Review senior editor Frank Meyer, a former Marxist and political philosopher by training. Meyer argued, first, that there is an objective moral order; second, that virtue consists in adhering to this moral order; third, that virtue that is coerced is not really virtue.

Fourth, it followed that in order for man to really be virtuous rather than to simply appear so, he must be free to make his own way—in the marketplace, in religion, and in life generally. He may head up the narrow path that leads to better things or down the wide and inviting path that doesn't.

Meyer wanted the take-away to be that free-market enthusiasts and traditionalists and religious conservatives could make common cause against Communism and Big Government. They could achieve traditionalist ends by libertarian means—by, for instance, cutting off government subsidies that encouraged irresponsible behavior.

The dark underbelly of Meyer's argument was that those traditionalists who were encouraging what they took to be virtue through government intervention were doing something misguided—or far worse. They were, in effect, trying to substitute conformity for actual virtue.

Fusionism had some problems, but it was a rigorous enough argument to be taken seriously, and it was an approach that might work politically, so Buckley seized on it. Fusionism or "libertarian conservatism," as it was sometimes clunkily called, would be the thing for Buckley and the other folks surrounding *National Review* to try out. They needed a guinea pig.

GOLDWATER'S CONSCIENCE

"We needed a national figure around whom to consolidate, and so we transfigured Barry Goldwater," Buckley wrote matter-of-factly in the preface to his penultimate book *Flying High*.[4]

"Transfigured" may have been overegging it. Conservative historian and Goldwater biographer Lee Edwards gives us the "before" snapshot: "Senator Barry Goldwater of Arizona was an outspoken conservative Republican who attracted national attention in the late fifties by calling the Eisenhower Administration's excessive spending a 'betrayal' of the public trust and for exposing trade union corruption in widely televised congressional hearings."[5]

Or maybe not. It's true that Buckley fastened onto Goldwater and promoted him relentlessly. He lent out Brent Bozell, who was then on the *National Review* payroll as the DC correspondent, to ghostwrite for Goldwater a pamphlet—something of a political manifesto.

Bozell turned out a manuscript that became one of the biggest political best sellers of all time, and certainly the best-selling fusionist text in the history of the known universe, *The Conscience of a Conservative*. "I am unaware," Goldwater stated in the manifesto, "of any moral virtue that is attached to my decision to confiscate the earnings of X and give them to Y."[6]

Buckley was one of the people who worked to draft Goldwater to enter into the race for the Republican presidential nomination in 1960. Goldwater eventually relented to let his name be considered, though he never thought he had a decent chance at winning the nomination or securing the vice presidential slot and was right about that. No matter. The real prize was 1964, and Buckley and nearly the entire *National Review* crew were pulling for him.

Through the early 1960s, Buckley used his magazine, his new weekly column syndicated by the *Washington Star*, and his regular speeches to promote the candidacy of Goldwater. As the 1964 campaign approached, *The Conscience of a Conservative* continued to sell hundreds of thousands of copies and to attract new, young followers to the Arizona senator, making him into something like the Ron Paul of the 1960s.

Then came JFK's fatal visit to Dallas on November 22, 1963, and Lyndon Johnson was president. Goldwater was convinced there was no chance that he could be elected over Johnson, and Buckley agreed with that judgment. It would be too traumatic for the American people to opt for three different presidents in less than a year.

Goldwater ran anyway, barely won a brutal primary fight with liberal Republican and New York governor Nelson Rockefeller, and ran one of the most honest, uncompromising general election campaigns the world has ever seen. Goldwater speechwriter Karl Hess called the campaign "an unbroken series of Goldwater decisions to say unpopular things simply because he thought they needed saying." He refused to pander to audiences, talked of drastically reducing the size and scope of the federal government, and said that he would approach the Cold War and its satellite skirmishes with a will to win.

That didn't sit well with political pundits, many of whom thought or outright said that he was crazy and dangerous. His remarks were constantly misrepresented in the press. One television advertisement, masterminded by Johnson aide and later PBS host Bill Moyers and released by the Johnson campaign, showed a little girl picking flowers, and then dying in a nuclear holocaust.

Anarchist philosopher Crispin Sartwell wrote in *Extreme Virtue* that Goldwater's "acceptance speech at the Republican National Convention . . . was a true act of defiance." Throughout the campaign, said Sartwell, "the basic attack on Goldwater was that he was a right-wing extremist." If he wanted to win the election, the Arizona senator "would have shown himself in the most moderate light possible, and there were elements of his record and rhetoric that would have made such a move plausible."

Goldwater weighed and rejected the moderate option, thinking it dishonest. Instead, said Sartwell, "he reacted rebelliously, extolling 'extremism in the pursuit of liberty' and condemning 'moderation in the pursuit of justice.'" Many of the more moderate Republicans at the convention "sat on their hands," and when Richard Nixon's wife, Pat, tried to rise with the crowd to cheer Goldwater, Dick wouldn't let her.[7]

The result was an electoral college bloodbath. Lyndon Johnson carried forty-four states for 486 votes to Goldwater's

52 votes, and even those votes were considered tainted, because a block of Deep Southern states only went Republican to protest the 1964 Civil Rights Act. Goldwater had opposed it for entirely nonracist, principled, constitutional reasons, but one doubts that is why the South started to go Republican for the first time since Reconstruction ended.

EMERGE SMILING

After they had put so much effort into Goldwater, the editors of *National Review* found themselves locked out of the actual 1964 general election campaign by Goldwater staffers. One reason may have been that Buckley not only agreed with Goldwater that he was unlikely to beat Johnson but also had had the effrontery to say so publicly.

Buckley addressed the Young Americans for Freedom on September 11. He told them that—off the record but later published in a collection of his speeches—he wanted to talk about "the impending defeat of Barry Goldwater." He said that it was important to talk about defeat now because it was vital that conservatives not be demoralized when they inevitably lost in November.

"On that day we must emerge smiling, confident in the knowledge that we weakened those walls [of the liberal establishment], that they will never again stand so firmly against us. On that day, we must be prepared to inform Lyndon Johnson that we too will continue," Buckley told the young conservatives.[8]

Fortunately, something near the tail end of the campaign gave conservatives unexpected reason to smile from ear to ear. Ronald Reagan, the staunchly anti-Communist former Screen Actors Guild president—but until then a devoted Democrat—taped a speech in favor of Goldwater that aired on October 27 titled "A Time for Choosing."

Reagan announced that he would be "crossing the aisle" to work for Goldwater's election. He complained about the crazy spending and inflation of the Johnson administration, and then he hit his stride.

"We're at war with the most dangerous enemy that has ever faced mankind in his long climb from the swamp to the stars, and it's been said if we lose that war, and in so doing lose this way of freedom of ours, history will record with the greatest astonishment that those who had the most to lose did the least to prevent its happening.

"Well I think it's time we ask ourselves if we still know the freedoms that were intended for us by the Founding Fathers," Reagan said, thus launching a political career that would prove, eventually, that Bill Buckley had been onto something.[9]

6

A POLITICAL
DISEASE RAGES

ill Buckley's famous 1965 campaign for mayor of New
York began as a joke. *National Review* was running an
article by Buckley on the reforms that New York City
should pursue. An editor suggested that they call attention to
this by putting "WFB for Mayor" on the cover. Then the magazine started getting calls and inquiries of where people might
sign up, and one thing led to another . . .

That's the nice official story, and it's partly true. But the
campaign wasn't quite that spontaneous. Buckley ended up running for mayor because of a feud he had with the very liberal
New York Republican John Lindsay. When Lindsay captured
the mayoral nomination of the Republican Party, Buckley
announced that he would stand for office on the Conservative
Party ticket, if they'd have him.

That caveat was a bit of false modesty. Buckley had played

an important role in founding New York's Conservative Party to oppose the liberal Republicanism of former governor Nelson Rockefeller and other liberal members of the GOP, including Jacob Javits, Irving Ives, and Lindsay. Of course they'd have him.

After Rockefeller had lost the Republican nomination in 1964, he, Lindsay, and fellow travelers in the GOP either didn't lift a finger to help Goldwater or else actively worked against him. That infuriated Buckley, and when Lindsay sought the endorsement of New York's Liberal Party on the ballot— thanks to New York's "fusion" election laws, multiple parties can endorse the same candidate—it was *on*.

The announcement of Buckley's candidacy on June 24, 1965, is legendary. Usually politicians will tell a story about how they decided to run for office as a way of building excitement. Buckley jumped right in. His direct, first words were "I propose to run for mayor of New York."[1]

He regretted that he could not do so as a Republican because the "Republican designation is not, in New York, available nowadays to anyone in the mainstream of Republican opinion." Buckley said he was running because the "main candidates" for mayor agreed that New York was in trouble but were "resolutely opposed to discussing the reasons why it is in crisis." He called the Republicans and the Democrats "symptomatic of a political disease that rages in New York, and threatens to contaminate Democratic government everywhere in the United States."

What was this democratic contagion? Buckley argued that

liberal solutions to governance were wrong, had stopped working, and were soon to be up against the wall. Voting bloc politics was starting to reach its absurd limits.

Every group wanted a handout or a special favor or exemption, and City Hall was finding it impossible to say no. This created additional problems because that money had to be raised, but people hate paying higher taxes, and they really don't like it when they see members of other groups benefiting more from the spoils system than they are.

It's a formula for perpetual grievance, Buckley warned, and worse. It creates crushing demands on the public treasury that local governments seek to solve by asking state and then federal governments to bail them out. Those governments often oblige the local polities by creating all kinds of programs to distribute money.

But that money comes with strings, requiring local governments to spend even more money and, remember, all of these funds must be raised from taxpayers *somewhere*. Government becomes an Ouroboros, eating its own tail.

SEETHING WITH FRUSTRATION

Buckley next spoke out against the crime problem in New York and proposed to actually do something about it. "We need . . . a much larger police force," he said, "enjoined to lust after the apprehension of criminals even as politicians lust after the acquisition of votes."

Cops also must be given a lot of latitude: "Under no circumstances must the police be encumbered by such political irons as civilian review boards." Those words alone got him out of dozens of traffic tickets in his lifetime. (Garry Wills told the story of the time that Buckley was giving Wills a ride on his scooter. They weren't wearing helmets. A cop pulled them over, saw that the driver was Bill Buckley, and waved them on.)

Buckley was willing to expand the police force by cutting elsewhere because "the protection of the individual against the criminal is the first and highest function of government" and "the failure of government to provide protection is nothing less than the failure of government." In fact, he even suggested that city government look into "providing some kind of indemnity for victims of certain kinds of crime." In other words, the government might compensate citizens it had failed to protect.

Then he took on what was then called "the Negro Problem." He started with a huge concession; namely, that "the ill-feeling that exists between the races in New York is due in part to a legacy of discrimination and injustice committed by the dominant ethnic groups. The white people owe a debt to the Negro people against whom we have discriminated for generations." And, "we should seek out ways to advance the Negro."

But—and you knew there was going to be a but—"to do this is not enough. We cannot help the Negro by adjourning our standards." He brought up the taboo subject of black illegitimacy and fingered some of his favorite villains: "In New York, the principal enemies of the Negro people are those demagogues of their own race before whom our politicians grovel."

He called out the black congressman from Harlem—Adam Clayton Powell Jr.—by name, as well as novelist and activist James Baldwin. (A report on the press conference said that Buckley, with his "Connecticut British accent," had pronounced it "Adam Clayton Powell June-ee-yore," making *junior* "the harshest word in the language.")

Buckley said that it was "the ultimate act of condescension" to "suppose that merely because a man is a Negro, one may not denounce him; that because he is a Negro it is hardly surprising that he is a poor husband, or an absent father, or a delinquent child." He pointed out that Baldwin "has said that the Negroes in Harlem who throw their garbage out in the streets do so as a form of social protest." Au contraire: "It is a much higher form of social protest to denounce such reasoning and the men who make it."

If elected, Buckley promised to reintroduce discipline into and decentralize New York's schools as well as offering "special financial inducements" for "first-rate teachers." He promised to defang the city's unions and order police to protect workers who cross picket lines, drastically scale back welfare payments and introduce a yearlong residency requirement before people could qualify, cut back on urban renewal schemes, and scrap the minimum wage.

He hoped that in the course of the campaign he would "succeed in introducing the other candidates to the New York that seethes with frustration while the politicians conduct their quadrennial charade." Then he stood for questions.

CONSERVATIVELY SPEAKING

The reporters must have been a little bit stunned. They asked the usual questions that journalists will ask of a candidate. Had he consulted with X? When was the primary? Who would he appoint? How many votes did he think his third-party bid could reasonably expect to get? What was his position on Y?

Beyond that, the basic thrust of their queries was, *Wait, are you serious?* Buckley's responses communicated his ongoing contempt for much of journalism and only fueled their cynicism:[2]

> REPORTER A: You listed your address as Wallach Point, Stamford, Connecticut. How long have you lived in New York?
>
> BUCKLEY: I have lived in New York longer than Bobby Kennedy did when he decided to run.
>
> REPORTER A: What is your address in New York?
>
> BUCKLEY: I don't give it out.
>
> REPORTER B: Are you in this campaign to win it, or are you in this campaign to . . . pick away at what you regard as Lindsay's fraud on the party?
>
> BUCKLEY: No. I am in this campaign to get as many votes as I can get, consistent with maintaining the

excellence of my position, so the decision, of course, is up to the people, not me. I will not adapt my views in order to increase my vote by ten people, as you have just seen.

REPORTER C: Do you want to be mayor, sir?

BUCKLEY: I have never considered it.

REPORTER D: Do you think it is something that should be considered?

BUCKLEY: Not necessarily. What is important is that certain points of view prevail. Whether you or I administer those points of view is immaterial to me, provided that you are a good administrator.

REPORTER E: But you are asking people to vote for you. If elected, will you serve?

BUCKLEY: If elected, I will serve.

REPORTER A: Do you think you have any chance of winning?

BUCKLEY: No.

REPORTER A: Why are you running?

BUCKLEY: I thought I had made that clear. I will read you my speech again if you like. It gives you about sixteen reasons why.

REPORTER F: Is this a press conference?

BUCKLEY: Whatever you make out of it.

REPORTER G: How many votes do you expect to get, conservatively speaking?

BUCKLEY: Conservatively speaking, one.

The *New York Times* editorialized dismissively, "William F. Buckley Jr., leading apostle of Goldwaterism on the Eastern Seaboard, has offered himself as the Conservative Party candidate for mayor. He regards New York as a city to be saved from crisis and, with his usual diffidence, himself as the man to do it. Whether New York is also ready for Mr. Buckley is another matter."

In a follow-up press conference, at his son's Benedictine boarding school, Portsmouth Abbey, a reporter put the question to Buckley squarely, "What would you do if you *were* elected?" And, again, Buckley toyed with the press. "Demand a recount," he said.

Press flaks for New York's Conservative Party were livid. The party's official position was that they stood a fighting chance. Buckley wrote in his great book about the campaign, *The Unmaking of a Mayor*, that Conservative press aide Kieran O'Doherty confidently predicted to several reporters Buckley would win the election "by a narrow margin."

When the vote totals came in that November, they fell . . . somewhat short of that. Though, on the plus side, Buckley's estimate turned out to be far too conservative:

Candidate	Vote
John Lindsay	44.9 percent
Abe Beame	40.9 percent
Bill Buckley	13.3 percent

LATER TO WIN?

Buckley ran for mayor when he knew he had no realistic chance of winning. Why would he do that? There were a lot of reasons. He thought he could use the platform to reach a larger audience with his message. He thought it might be fun and be good grist for a book. After Goldwater had gone down to defeat, Buckley wanted somebody—anybody—to carry the conservative torch. He hoped to pull enough Republican votes away from Lindsay to cost him the election.

Looking back on the race, Buckley campaign manager Neal Freeman remembered most Buckley's "courage, both physical and moral." He explained that in the politics of the 1960s "the stakes seemed to be higher. People who stirred passions in the public arena tended to attract not just criticism but gunfire." Freeman initially kept a file of the threats, but he soon discovered that "Bill was never interested."[3]

Election night found Buckley in a foul, foul mood, and he had a hard time, for once, groping for something to say to supporters. Of course, he didn't win. That much he knew going in, and he had managed to defang the loss by repeatedly predicting it. However, he didn't even manage to cost Lindsay the election.

The reason for Lindsay's victory was simple but unexpected. Buckley's conservative message found a more receptive audience in traditional Democratic constituencies than it did among the city's Republicans. So Buckley managed to take more votes away from Abe Beame, and John Lindsay became mayor of New York.

Lindsay proved to be an awful mayor. The transit workers struck the first day he took office in January 1966. The city didn't have any bus or subway service for two weeks, and the union managed to get most of its demands met. That weakened Lindsay from the start and made any of his halting attempts to control spending into mostly futile efforts.

Not that Lindsay was gung ho about fiscal restraint. He greatly expanded welfare programs and grew the city's bureaucracy. By the time he left office, crime and high taxes had driven about a million New Yorkers out of the city. Historian Vincent Cannato titled his book about the Lindsay years *The Ungovernable City*, and that certainly seemed to be the case. New York City almost filed for bankruptcy in 1975 and had to be bailed out by the federal government.

Buckley's candidacy set certain things in motion that helped New York recover from the crisis. It nudged the Republican Party in the direction of law and order and fiscal sanity. Lindsay managed to win a second term as mayor in 1969 as a Liberal, not a Republican. The next year, Bill's brother James Buckley ran for a Senate seat as a Conservative against both Democrat Richard Ottinger and liberal Republican Charles Goodell. Jim Buckley won the three-way race and captured the Republican nomination in the next election.

The conservative threat pushed the politics of the state to the right for the other parties as well. Democrat Daniel Patrick

Moynihan beat Jim Buckley in 1976, but only after defeating the very liberal feminist Bella Abzug in the Democratic primary. Abzug then went on to lose in the Democratic mayoral primary to the much more conservative Ed Koch.

And in 1993, Republican Rudy Giuliani—Rudy Giuliani!—was also endorsed by the Liberal Party in his successful bid for mayor of New York City.

7

SNAKES ON A
CAMPAIGN

ritics have intimated that Bill Buckley used his run for
mayor to launch his television career. Buckley claimed
the opposite was true, that the mayoral race actually slowed him down. It's very nearly plausible. He had been
approached about doing a public affairs show and had to put
those plans on hold through most of 1965 as he made his doomed
run at City Hall.

Buckley certainly wasn't hurting for speaking gigs or serious media attention before the political bug bit. In fact, politics
could easily have derailed his media career. Bill planned to
contest Bobby Kennedy's New York Senate seat in 1970. That
would have meant abandoning his new television show and perhaps his regular, now thrice-weekly syndicated column.

After RFK was shot, Bill decided to let his brother Jim,
who had parachuted in from Maine to help Bill run for mayor,

run for the Senate seat instead. Bill penned one of the most bizarre endorsements for Jim ever conceived of by man.

In the pages of the *Newsday*, Bill made the case for his brother based on his unique character. Jim, said Bill, was the "only person I have ever known who has no enemies." This wasn't because his older brother lacked opinions or resolve, but because there was "something about him that has always persuaded everyone with whom he has contact that his fairness is, in a sense, a tribute even to those who are the immediate victims of his fairness."[1]

For instance, say that Jim was the witness to an accident between his best friend and the Black Panther Party's Eldridge Cleaver "and Jim saw that Cleaver had the green light." Jim would testify to that in court and Jim's friend, even if he believed that Jim was wrong, "would—somehow—bear no resentment at all against Jim."

On a related note, Bill launched into the story of the time that Jim convinced his father to invite Jim's biology teacher to Great Elm, in Connecticut, for the summer. The Buckley children spent what would have been their free time "either in discussing the singular virtues, ecological and moral, of leaving snakes unmolested; or in making graven images in plaster of Paris of various leaves taken from otherwise innocent trees; or in helping to build cages for what would become . . . the next largest zoo north of the Bronx."

When Will Buckley got home from a stay in Europe, he very quickly released the zooish captives. The point of the story, according to Bill, was that "gruesome though [that summer] was," somehow the Buckley children didn't "blame it on Jim, though there was never any doubt that he was *personally and with malice aforethought responsible.*" But the real point of the story was to set up an even more bizarre revelation or possible tall tale.

Bill told the story of Martha, Jim's pet boa constrictor, left over from their animal-house days. At Yale, Jim would take Martha with him to class. The snake "wound 'round his neck, then down his sleeve, to the shirt cuff," where she would either sleep or listen to the lecture. The dean of Jim's college got wind of this and ordered him to remove the snake from campus. Jim had brought Martha with him to another Buckley family residence in South Carolina and intended to leave her there while he attended college.

Then, only minutes before he needed to leave for the train to get back to college, Jim told everybody that Martha had somehow got out of her cage. "Distress does not do justice to the state of mind of those of us, young and old, who were *not* leaving the house in order to go back to the safety of Yale," Bill wrote.

They worried that Martha might just mistake one of them for Jim in the middle of the night and snuggle up a little too tight. This frightened them "since boa constrictors do not fool around when they embrace you." Yet "even after *that*," wrote Bill, "we didn't hate Jimmy." And the voters shouldn't hate him either.

ADVERTISEMENTS FOR HIMSELF

It is technically true that Bill Buckley delayed his television-hosting career to run for mayor. But it is undeniably true that he milked the mayoral run for all it was worth.

On August 4, 1965, Buckley traveled to Washington DC and held a press conference at the National Press Club head-quarters. The reason given for the trip was to make a point about federal overreach into the affairs of state and local gov-ernments. And Buckley eventually got around to complaining about that, but the real purpose of the event was greater public-ity through novelty.

Rather than take questions from reporters, Buckley inter-viewed himself—literally. He stood at the podium and pretended to be two people, turning his neck from one side to the other as he changed personas—from Bill Buckley the interviewer to Bill Buckley the political candidate, and back. He began:

> BUCKLEY-AS-INTERVIEWER: Mr. Buckley, why are
> you running for mayor of New York?
> BUCKLEY-AS-CANDIDATE: Because nobody else is
> who matters.

And of course Buckley asked himself the follow-up, "What do you mean 'who matters'?" Much of the Q and A set up his stump speech, but the questions weren't all softballs, by any means, and a few of the exchanges gave a hint of what he'd be like as a television host. To wit:

INTERVIEWER: Why didn't you run in the Republican primary?

CANDIDATE: Why didn't Martin Luther King run for governor of Alabama?

INTERVIEWER: For one thing, he isn't a resident of Alabama.

CANDIDATE: That could be arranged.

INTERVIEWER: Are you comparing yourself to Martin Luther King?[2]

He answered no, but those sort of barbed, short, back-and-forths would be typical of the spirited exchanges on *Firing Line*. Look at the mayoral press conference, and you get the sense that Buckley was giving it a dry run to see how it was received.

You also get the sense that he thought it a roaring success. He used the self-interrogation to introduce his book *The Unmaking of a Mayor*. In Buckley's final 2008 novel, *The Rake*, roguish lead Ruben Castle does something similar though even more over-the-top. Castle is a senator, presidential hopeful, and former anti-Vietnam student activist. He is scheduled to debate a famous general about Vietnam before a college audience, but then the general takes ill.

Castle doesn't want to cancel, and he also doesn't want to be robbed of the opportunity to debate. Rather than simply speechify to the students, he decides to play both parts—the pro-war general and the antiwar senator—and debate himself.

The gesture is so well received that it nearly carries him into the White House.

NOT READY FOR PBS

Firing Line debuted in April 1966. It was a very different show in the early days from the show that it became. It is remembered now as a forum for civilized debate and long conversation by the attention span–shortened standards of modern television.

Buckley's show eventually found a home on PBS and lasted longer than any other American public affairs show—thirty-three years and more than fifteen hundred episodes. In the early years, it was broadcast on commercial television and was more like the intellectual prize fight of the week, with Bill Buckley going up against—and bloodying—famous liberals.

The first guest was Norman Thomas, six-time presidential candidate for the Socialist Party of America. When people use the phrase "grand old man of the Left," Thomas is the kind of person they have in mind. By the time he faced Buckley on *Firing Line*, Thomas was two years from the grave and nearly blind. Buckley had to signal that it was time for a break by touching him on the arm.

Thomas was a dedicated socialist, but not a toady for the Soviet Union, and Buckley later admitted that he might have overdone it in arguing with the man, though he insisted that Thomas in his prime was "a highly truculent debater." Thomas had supported the Korean War, and Buckley used that against him. The two got into it over Vietnam. Buckley asked Thomas if his change of heart, from supporting war in Korea to opposing war in Vietnam, was "a function of age or is it a function of what?"[3]

Neal Freeman went from Buckley's mayoral campaign to *Firing Line*. He has said that Buckley hated the name of the show but was stuck with it by early financial backers. Buckley comforted himself that after the initial thirteen-episode season, the show probably wouldn't be renewed.

One great irony is that without government-sponsored public television, it would not have lasted nearly so long. The show attracted a dedicated following but not one large enough to survive for a long time on commercial television.

Freeman told me that his favorite episode from the pugilistic phase of the show was Buckley's debate with James Wechsler, editor of the *New York Post*. *Wait a minute,* you might be thinking, *Why would he be arguing with the* New York Post?

Freeman anticipated your question and explained, "In those mid-60s days, long after its founding by Alexander Hamilton, and long before its acquisition by Rupert Murdoch, the *Post* was a sharp, combative lefty paper, and Jimmy Wechsler was the smartest, toughest lefty in town. When our boy Bill cuffed Wechsler around for a long sixty minutes, we knew we were on our way: the *Firing Line* franchise had been established."[4]

There is a certain undeniable attraction to those early shows. *Firing Line*, with its bare set—usually just Buckley and an opponent or two sitting in swivel chairs, Buckley clutching his stopwatch, clipboard, and pen; rigorous introductions, and enforced manners (Buckley called everybody by honorifics and expected the same) was one of the purest exchanges of ideas television audiences ever witnessed.

It was formal, and it was brutal, so much so that several prominent politicians refused to go on *Firing Line*. The question was put to Buckley, "Why doesn't Bobby Kennedy go on your show?" "Why does baloney fear the grinder?" he replied.

It's interesting to listen in on some of those early exchanges, when Buckley really let it rip. With Thomas, he interrupted his guest to tell him "something that will displease you most," which was that "people can be made to live like animals" under Communism. Buckley thereby insinuated that was exactly what Thomas secretly desired.

DEMONSTRATION OF SINCERITY

If that's all *Firing Line* was—a smart, opinionated host running roughshod over his guests—then it would be remembered as a more literate precursor to *Crossfire*-like cable shows and conservative talk radio. Buckley wasn't always happy with how the early shows came off. So he changed things up considerably. He sought a wider variety of guests and topics, and tried to be less abrasive.

It made for some of the best television ever. Buckley only partially captured this in his 1989 book *On the Firing Line*.

In that volume, he gives us Timothy Leary preaching that America was founded on the motto "Sorry, George the Third, we're dropping out," and saying to Buckley, "I consider myself to be much more conservative than you."

Buckley gave us Muhammad Ali arguing for his sincerity in converting to the Nation of Islam. Even before the draft board tried to reclassify him and send him to Vietnam, Ali said, he divorced his first wife because "she wouldn't wear her dresses long."

Ali spelled out exactly how much money that cost him: "It cost me two hundred and fifty thousand dollars. I'm paying twelve hundred dollars a month now in alimony. I paid nearly ninety-six thousand dollars in lawyers' fees. Now if that's not sincerity, I don't know what is."

And Buckley concurred: "I can't think of any other attempt by anyone, anywhere, in any circumstances, more eloquent to demonstrate his sincerity, than Muhammad Ali that afternoon."[5]

But in his book Buckley doesn't give us certain things from *Firing Line* that made the show so unique: The exchange with Huey Newton about the American Revolution excerpted in the first chapter of this book. Or an older Jack Kerouac laying into musician Ed Sanders of the Fugs. Or Allen Ginsberg chanting the Hare Krishna. We see a picture of Kurt Vonnegut alongside Norman Mailer but don't hear from the old, chain-smoking, mustachioed yarn spinner.

Because of the state of technology at the time, Buckley really couldn't give us those things. The transcripts of *Firing*

Line will get you only so far. Some of it you have to see to believe. In 1989 there wasn't a good way to give potential audiences serious access to a television show's voluminous archive.

With the advent of YouTube, DVDs, and Internet shopping sites, it is now much easier to see what all the fuss was about. The Hoover Institution has put together a large archive of Buckley's shows. Information, clips, transcripts, and such can be found at http://hoohila.stanford.edu/firingline/.

Many of the episodes are available for purchase through sites such as Amazon.com and, more important, clips of these shows that zero in on choice moments can be found on YouTube. Check it out.

STAY PLASTERED

Firing Line and his syndicated column "On the Right" changed Buckley's ambitions. His first few books—*God and Man at Yale, McCarthy and His Enemies*, and *Up from Liberalism*—were treatments of serious subjects, spaced several years apart. And his magazine was a serious journal of ideas, albeit one with a sense of humor.

In 1963 he had planned to write another serious book of ideas called *The Revolt Against the Masses*, but he couldn't wrap his head around it. He wanted to take another pass at it in 1964, but the Goldwater effort, speaking, and columnizing ate up much of his time. In 1965 he ran for mayor. In 1966 he published *The Unmaking of a Mayor* and launched *Firing Line*. He started to regularly collect his columns and essays, along with bits of correspondence, and publish those as books, to great commercial success.

Buckley would write several other fine full-length books, but he didn't think he had anything new to say, politically. Conservatism was about the application of timeless truths, and he no longer lacked for outlets to promote those truths. He had *National Review*, access to most newspaper markets, and an electronic invitation into people's living rooms through *Firing Line*.

Given his ever-extending reach, it probably shouldn't surprise that Buckley's most famous television exchange was not part of his television show. In 1968, he had contracted with ABC to give commentary on the Republican and Democratic conventions. He appeared opposite the expatriate gay left-wing novelist Gore Vidal, and it was obvious from the opening bell that the two loathed each other. Buckley made fun of Vidal's novels. Vidal threw any charge at Buckley that he thought might stick.

When the two started arguing over the protests and riots and police brutality that surrounded the Democratic convention in Chicago, well, readers would greatly benefit from a trip to YouTube at this point, because a transcript has to order items in a sequence, and it can't convey the physical situation well. Type in "buckley vidal debate" and then watch that as you read:

VIDAL: I assume it is the point of view of American democracy that you can express any point of view you want.

BUCKLEY: And some of the people [the protesters] were pro-Nazi.

VIDAL: Shut up a minute.

BUCKLEY: No, I won't. . . . I am for ostracizing people who egg on other people to shoot American Marines and American soldiers. [Protesters had unfurled a Vietcong flag in Hyde Park.] I know you don't because you don't have any sense of identification—

VIDAL: As far as I am concerned, the only sort of pro- or crypto-Nazi that I can think of is yourself. Failing that I would only say we can't have the right of assembly if we're—

MODERATOR: Let's not call names.

BUCKLEY: Now, listen, you queer, stop calling me a crypto-Nazi—

MODERATOR: Let's stop, let's stop—

BUCKLEY: —or I'll sock you in your . . . face

VIDAL: Oh Bill, you're so extraordinary.

MODERATOR: Gentlemen, let's stop calling names.

BUCKLEY: And you'll stay plastered. [*Leans over, clearly thinking about socking Vidal on the air.*] Let the author of *Myra Breckinridge* go back to his pornography and stop making allusions of Nazism to somebody who was in the last war and fought the Nazis.

Now, *that's* television!

A New Literary History of America (2009) tries to place the event in its proper historical context. Buckley and Vidal's "adversarial commentary slipped out of control and descended to ugly name calling, mirroring the tumult in Chicago and the nervous energy of the sixties zeitgeist, unhinged by serial assassinations and a war that the United States was not winning in Vietnam."

You see, "if protesters and the police could not contain their political furor in 1968 then neither could these middle-aged intellectuals, dressed for television in respectable suits and ties."[6]

BUCKLEY V. *PLAYBOY*

Before we abandon the swinging 1960s for the grim '70s, we should pause to consider one outrage that Buckley managed to inspire among many conservative Christians. It was over the fact that he allowed himself to be interviewed by and wrote for *Playboy*.

Buckley initially claimed that he did so because he wanted to reach the magazine's large audience. He famously quipped that's where he had to write if he wanted his son to read him. Buckley ultimately stopped writing for the magazine because he concluded, from the paucity of responses, that most people really don't read it for the articles after all.

All the while he contributed to the magazine, in his other writings Buckley attacked *Playboy* and the "Playboy philosophy" the magazine promoted. He used a long interview that appeared in the magazine to open his collection of essays *Inveighing We Will Go*. In that interview, he was asked what he thought could be done to "keep the population down." He retorted: "Get people to stop reading *Playboy*."

Then there was the poetry of it. When *Playboy* asked Buckley how he could "be so sure" that his theological dogmas wouldn't "crumble sooner or later," Buckley reached deep into the Old Testament and found a passage from the book of Job: "I know that my Redeemer liveth."[7]

Finally, while most readers didn't read *Playboy* for the articles, one very important young man did. At the Portsmouth Abbey conference on Buckley, Father Damian Kearney, who had been the housemaster over Bill's son, Christopher, reported that "while Chris was a student, I was checking the rooms during study period and found Chris openly and unashamedly reading a copy of *Playboy*, a magazine that was strictly taboo but enjoyed an underground popularity among many of the students. He then calmly announced that he was reading his father's article which had just appeared in the current issue."

Father Kearney didn't know quite what to say to that at the time. In 2009 he called it "evidence of yet another side of Buckley's multifaceted personality and perhaps an indication of the catholicity of his tastes."[8] That's one way of putting it.

RACE, SEX, ROME,
AND AYN RAND

I n August 1957, *National Review* ran its most infamous unsigned editorial, titled "Why the South Must Prevail."[1] It argued that "the white community in the South is entitled to take such measures as are necessary to prevail, politically and culturally, in areas which it does not predominate numerically" because "for the time being, it is the advanced race" and the "claims of civilization supersede those of universal suffrage."

Bill Buckley biographer John Judis tells us that Bill not only approved but also penned that editorial, which "crossed the line between constitutionalism and racism."[2] This defense of the subjugation of blacks proved indefensible—not in the long run of American history, but right away. Buckley was forced to eat some Jim Crow in the very next issue.

Brent Bozell pointed out in the pages of *National Review* that the position of the editors flatly contradicted the Fifteenth

Amendment to the United States Constitution, which the magazine claimed to revere. The amendment reads:

1. The right of citizens of the United States to vote shall not be denied or abridged by the United States or by any State on account of race, color, or previous condition of servitude.
2. The Congress shall have power to enforce this article by appropriate legislation.

National Review then adopted the almost comic position that the problem wasn't that the Negro might get the vote, *per se*, but that too many people have the right to vote, period. If the South wanted to deny the uneducated Negro the vote, then it should "do so by enacting laws that apply equally to blacks and whites, thus living up to the spirit of the Constitution and the letter of the Fifteenth Amendment."[3]

It was an unworkable proposal, nonracist in theory but bound to encourage all the wrong kinds of mischief. Poor, white Southerners were not going to allow themselves to be disenfranchised simply to deny blacks the vote. And whatever the law read, white Southern election officials would be much more likely to deny the vote to uneducated black folks than to fellow whites. In fact, that's precisely how mandatory literacy laws were usually applied.

The original editorial and the editorial compromise hamstrung Buckley. He tried to argue for the disenfranchisement of both blacks and whites in a debate with black author James

Baldwin before the Cambridge Student Union in 1965. Buckley was nearly laughed off the stage for that.

It damaged his reputation and the reputation of his magazine. Anytime Buckley or *National Review* claimed that they opposed civil rights legislation or affirmative action or forced busing or other racially tinged programs for constitutional or prudential reasons, critics would point back to that one poisonous editorial and say that these other justifications simply served as a sophisticated cover for racism.

Bill didn't worry about placating critics, exactly, but he did go extra hard on actual segregationists. When former segregationist, former Alabama governor, and third-party presidential candidate George Wallace appeared on *Firing Line* in January 1968, things got a bit heated.

Buckley insinuated that Wallace was still a segregationist. Wallace accused Buckley of wanting to slight the poor. Buckley "answered him, mock-solemnly 'I hate the poor,'" but that definitely "didn't work." Wallace continued to duck Buckley's barbs and ultimately, Buckley admitted, "out pointed me in our exchange."

Wallace managed this feat, said Buckley, because in 1968 the "general feeling among political conservatives . . . was that George Wallace was a social pariah. I shared that feeling and clearly acted as if I did." Buckley's antagonism to Wallace was "rooted in the great event of 1963 whence emerged as the most adamant American political figure standing in the way of desegregation" by sending in state troopers to keep blacks out of the University of Alabama.[4]

So he came around with little protest on the question of seg-regation, but that didn't mean Buckley was about to be any less controversial. In his Cambridge debate with Baldwin, Buckley complained that the only way to have an honest back-and-forth was to treat Baldwin the same way he would "a white man," and he often attacked black intellectuals and black leadership for a variety of failings. For this reason Buckley's mayoral bid drew charges of racism.

Buckley was occasionally critical of Reverend Martin Luther King Jr. but usually afforded him some respect, because he agreed with the reverend's powerful religious message about the brotherhood of man. In the 1980s, Buckley broke with some conservatives to endorse the idea of making King's birthday a federal holiday.

He didn't take it so easy on some other black leaders. In 1991, when President George H. W. Bush announced the nomination of Clarence Thomas to a seat on the Supreme Court, Buckley wrote that over the next twenty-four hours, "[DC Delegate to Congress] Eleanor Holmes Norton was everywhere, National Public Radio, PBS—I am fairly certain she was talking about the shortcomings of Judge Thomas to the sleepy bartender at five in the morning."[5]

WHAT'S THE *MATER*?

The second most controversial editorial that *National Review* ever published concerned a papal letter, or "encyclical," written by John XXIII, released in May 1961, called *Mater et Magistra* (Mother and Teacher). The letter argued against Western colonialism and for the moral necessity of rich countries coming to the aid of the world's poor.[6]

The thing that exercised the editors of *National Review* was what it left out. The editorial set up the issue by saying that the encyclical could either become central to Church teaching in the future or "become the source of embarrassed explanations." It argued for the second option, calling the encyclical a "venture in triviality at this particular time in history." After all, the most pressing concern for Church and state was "surely the demonic successes of the Communists," of which there was "scant mention" in the letter. (Communism was alluded to in the twenty-five-thousand-word document, but not by name.)

As for concern for the world's poor, the editors commended "the extraordinary material well-being that such free economic systems as Japan's, West Germany's, and our own are generating," and complained that the pope had paid "insufficient notice" to the poverty-alleviating power of capitalism. Rather than lecture the world's rich nations, in other words, the pope should tell the poor nations to stop standing in the way of their people's attempts to better themselves.

They tried to avoid charges of anticlericalism by invoking the bishops. *National Review* predicted that "in the years ahead, *Mater et Magistra* will suffer from comparison with the American Catholic Bishops' hierarchy of emphases, in their notable annual message of November 1960."

They might have got away with that, but the next issue of *National Review* included a brief item. It read in full: "Going the rounds in conservative Catholic circles: 'Mater, si; Magistra, no.'" (Mother, yes; Teacher, no.) It was a joke, a play on words on the Latin American revolutionary taunt *"Cuba si, Yanqui no,"* but many Catholics treated it as no laughing *Mater*.

The Jesuit journal *America* editorialized that *National Review* was flirting with disloyalty to Rome and "owes its Catholic readers and journalistic allies an apology." Editor and priest Thurston Davis wrote that it "takes a daring young man to characterize a papal document as 'a venture in triviality.' From long practice on the high wire, Mr. Buckley possesses that kind of daring." Message: he's set himself up for a great fall. *America* found the controversy so repugnant, in fact, that it refused to run *National Review*'s ads.

Several writers for Catholic diocesan newspapers followed suit ("This is the kind of stuff from which seedling schisms sprout," said one), and the story was taken up in the popular press. One cartoon featured Buckley, Martin Luther–like, nailing the words *Magistra, no* to the Vatican's doors. *Time* magazine titled its article about the virtues of the encyclical "Teacher, yes; Mother, no."

Buckley responded that sometimes a joke is just a joke, and in this case it wasn't even his witticism. The young writer and ex-Jesuit seminarian Garry Wills had told it to him, and Buckley couldn't resist. He apologized for that offense but maintained, first, that *National Review* was not an official Catholic journal just because it had a Catholic editor (or else, by analogy, John F. Kennedy would have made the entire U.S. government Catholic); second, that even if it were Catholic, the magazine would have been within its rights to question the wisdom of the Vatican issuing that particular message at that particular point in history; and third, that Catholic liberals were opportunistically blowing up a minor disagreement to damn their political opponents as heretics.

He may have been right about all of the above, but with his lack of deference to authority, Buckley was displaying his Irish Protestant roots. John Judis edged up to this when he said Buckley's religion "was rooted in his conception of God, rather than Rome's authority," though Bill did think the two were ultimately related. On an episode of *Firing Line*, Buckley debated organized religion with his Yale philosophy prof Paul Weiss. It took a fun turn:

> WEISS: I don't remember when God organized religion. Is there any time when *God* organized religion?
>
> BUCKLEY: Well the situation was like this—there was God and there was Peter, you see—
>
> WEISS: I thought they were distinct.
>
> BUCKLEY: They are.
>
> WEISS: Oh, good! Now, then—what?
>
> BUCKLEY: Well, then, a church was organized—
>
> WEISS: Fine.

BUCKLEY: By God.
WEISS: He did that?
BUCKLEY: Uh huh.[7]

The *Mater et Magistra* flap left a few scars. Buckley had been known as a dutiful son of the Church. Several liberal Catholic reviewers of *God and Man at Yale* had called him misguided but not disloyal. In his responses to Catholic critics, Buckley stressed that his non-Catholic magazine had, at most, taken issue with non-infallible papal teachings—that is, teachings that the Catholic Church itself does not claim are entirely free from error.

Yet the criticism that Buckley cared more about his political positions than his religious orthodoxy lingered, and smarted.

STRONG WILLS

One problem that the 1960s presented Buckley was that religious orthodoxy itself seemed to come unstuck. The Second Vatican Council changed the Catholic Church in important ways. Catholics believe in the progressive development of doctrine. Some of the new developments took a while to work themselves out.

Previously, the Church had been all too willing to meddle in matters of state and use government as a tool to enforce religious orthodoxy because "error" enjoyed no rights. The documents of Vatican II said several things. Among them was that the Church would no longer use the state to enforce religion.

The reasoning behind that position was interesting, and its fusionist implications must have made Buckley's ears perk right up. Before the Council, it was understood that believers could be divided roughly between those who took holy orders and those who did not.

Bishops, priests, nuns, and maybe even deacons—the "religious" was the technical term for them—were expected to be especially virtuous and could become celebrated saints. Everybody else was expected to do the best they could. For the second group—the laity—extra laws were sometimes needed as a guardrail to keep them from veering off the narrow path.

Vatican II said that all believers, not just the religious, could be and should be saints. Part of being a saint means living a life of heroic virtue, and that virtue should be freely chosen. This new optimism changed the way the Church hierarchy approached its own worshipers as much as it did its approach to secular governance. Mass in Latin was discouraged and then effectively banned, in favor of Masses in local tongues. The priest no longer faced away from the audience when he was consecrating the host. People were made to shake hands with complete strangers.

When it came to matters Catholic in the 1960s, the two greatest influences on Bill Buckley were Brent Bozell and Garry Wills. It's a slight exaggeration, but I've taken to thinking of them as the cartoonish angel and devil on Buckley's shoulders.

That isn't to say that Bozell was always right—he founded the rigorist quasi-cult called the Sons of Thunder and suffered from a severe bipolar disorder—but that almost all of Buckley's bad ideas about religion came from Garry Wills.

Wills, you'll recall, was the person who supplied Buckley with the quip that got him into so much trouble with Catholic liberals. As the '60s dragged into the '70s, Wills became more liberal in both politics and religion, and until the two had a serious falling-out, Wills influenced Buckley greatly.

It was because of the influence of Wills that Buckley embraced Mass in English and became a lector at his local Catholic Church. The experience nearly drove Buckley mad. After three years of trying to go along with the new Mass, Buckley resigned his position and sought out one of the few churches that offered the Latin Mass of his youth.

We can also detect the influence of Wills on an infamous column that Buckley wrote in 1966, saying that the "principal meaning of Vatican II is that other men must be left free to practice the dictates of their own conscience." If those "other religions and other individuals do not believe that under certain circumstances abortion is wrong," then it would contradict the Vatican's new position to involve itself with abortion laws.[8]

As with the segregationist editorial, Bozell stepped in and took issue with Buckley's position. And as he had done before, Buckley quickly reconsidered and relented. He endorsed the position that abortion was not a "Catholic issue," but rather a human rights issue.

In much of his writing about abortion after the conscience kerfuffle, Buckley stressed that science clearly showed us that there was a unique human life in the womb from the earliest days of pregnancy, and that the protection of innocent human life from violence was a bedrock commitment of all civilized nations. In 1974, his brother Jim introduced in the Senate, and Bill supported, a human life amendment to the United States Constitution that would have overturned *Roe v. Wade*.

"A" IS AYN

"You are too intelligent to believe in God," were the first words best-selling novelist Ayn Rand uttered to Buckley when they met in the early 1950s, according to Buckley. It was a flattering opening from a woman who was not normally given over to that sort of thing, and for a while the two got along tolerably well.

Yet by the time Rand died in 1982, the two hadn't been on speaking terms for decades. In an obituary in *National Review*, Buckley began by stating the obvious: "Ayn Rand is dead." Then he got to the point: "So, incidentally is the philosophy she sought to launch; it was, in fact, stillborn."[9] That may or may not be true. He certainly tried to throttle it.

Rand's program, spelled out in her pro-capitalist novels *Fountainhead* and *Atlas Shrugged*, in essays, and in talks to her small group of dedicated followers, was called "Objectivism." Her fledgling philosophy celebrated the glories of free enterprise and diabolized those who would fetter entrepreneurial genius with taxation, regulation, and small-mindedness. It might have appealed to Buckley were it not for two things. First was Rand's crucial materialistic demand: give up your God. Second was the increasingly cultlike nature of her following.

Buckley would certainly have been on board for a stout defense of capitalism, but Rand stood as a direct challenge to the kind of philosophical and political coalition that he was trying to build. He believed freedom was God given. That's why Christians should support capitalism, that's why capitalists should support religion, and that's why everybody should oppose the Communists. She thought that formulation was absurd.

Buckley argued that in the battle between individualism and collectivism, conservatives were on the side of the angels. Rand argued that there were no angels and that a belief in angels was a denial of objective reality and thus wrong and contemptible. (She expelled one student from her inner circle not because he believed in God but because his wife did, and he wouldn't denounce her.)

Buckley commissioned for *National Review* and ran a scathing review in 1957 by Whittaker Chambers of Rand's most ambitious novel, *Atlas Shrugged*. Chambers wrote that "any ordinarily sensible head could not possibly take it seriously." He called it a "remarkably silly book" with a "preposterous" storyline that cast a small group of self-interested industrialists as the "children of light" against politicians and plebes as "looters" and "children of darkness."

Chambers speculated that actual flesh-and-blood "children probably irk the author and make her uneasy," and said that her misanthropy runs much deeper than that: "From almost any page of *Atlas Shrugged*, a voice can be heard, from painful necessity, commanding: 'To a gas chamber—go!'"[10] It isn't too hard to figure out why Rand stopped talking to Buckley after that.

Almost everybody who reads the Chambers review will think it's unfair. A better question would be, was Chambers onto something? I think so. In an August 2002 column in the London *Spectator*, Michael Harrington made the case that Rand's most celebrated novel is really a "long, inverted and malevolent parody of the New Testament."

In the Gospels, said Harrington, Jesus "used divine power to heal the sick." In *Atlas Shrugged*, Rand hero John Galt "withholds scientific knowledge knowing that the sick will die." Contra Jesus, who "sent his disciples into the world to heal and preach and save," Galt "calls his disciples in from the world in order to bring it down in ruin."

"There is a kind of Day of Judgment in *Atlas Shrugged*," explained Harrington, "in which Galt addresses the American people, having taken temporary control of the radio stations. He says, in effect, 'You are in a terrible mess; it is all your own fault, and it is no use thinking that I am going to lift a finger to help you.'"[11] Not gas chambers exactly, but pretty close.

The possibility that a pro-capitalist, godless, pitiless ideology could gain a large group of adherents clearly disturbed

Bill Buckley. He published the Chambers review, tried to bury objectivism with Rand's obituary, and then came back to lob more dirt with the 2003 novel *Getting It Right*, which dwelt on the details and the scandals of the group of followers that surrounded Rand. It was a warning to future would-be followers to stay away.

9

IDEAL CONSERVATIVE
PRESIDENT

John Judis has argued that you can divide Bill Buckley's public career into two distinct phases: the wilderness years and the establishment years. In the first phase, he was a dedicated, serious critic of the political and cultural establishment—a prophet crying out in the wilderness. In the second phase, Buckley was part of that establishment—more like King Ahab's court prophets.

The best evidence for this is Bill Buckley's on-again, off-again support for Richard Nixon. Leading up to the 1968 election, Buckley told reporters that he would back "the most right, viable candidate," with the emphasis on "viable." That was a departure from *National Review*'s and his position that it would be best to hold out for a real conservative. Recall that no endorsements were forthcoming in 1956 and 1960.

He could hold the original all-or-nothing position because

he didn't view the Democratic Party as an unambiguous threat. Both parties had been a hodgepodge of liberals and conservatives and, if anything, it was the voting base of the Democratic Party that proved more susceptible to conservative arguments, as his run for New York mayor showed. Frequently, legislation that conservatives disliked would be kept bottled up in committee by conservative Southern Democratic committee chairmen. But things were changing.

After the LBJ landslide, after the flood of new federal programs that were rammed through the overwhelmingly Democratic Congress, after the buildup but endless dithering over how to fight the Vietnam War, Bill Buckley thought it was important to back a winner who could at least put the brakes on. And he came around to the belief that the man who could do that was the man his magazine had declined to endorse in 1960: Richard Nixon.

Buckley started saying nice things about him and then endorsed Nixon in 1968. He threw the weight of *National Review* behind Nixon and didn't do anything to encourage the "draft Reagan" movement at the Republican convention that year. It might have worked. Buckley had some pull with conservatives in the Republican Party, and they weren't wild about renominating the losing candidate from two election cycles ago.

As it was, Nixon was forced to cut a deal with South Carolina senator—and recent party switcher—Strom Thurmond, that gave Thurmond veto power over the vice presidential selection in return for keeping the Southern delegates in Nixon's camp. That's how the Republicans ended up nominating Spiro Agnew for vice president. Maryland delegate Louise Gore (a Republican relative of future Democratic vice president Al Gore) literally led Agnew by the hand to meet Thurmond and made the case for him, and then told Nixon that Agnew had passed the Thurmond test.

Buckley could have at least demanded more for his support. By then, he and Reagan had become friends, and Reagan had gone on from speechifying for Goldwater to winning the California governorship in a million-vote landslide in 1966. Nixon had attempted to use that office as a springboard to his political comeback in 1962, lost the election, held a bitter press conference, and moved to New York. And Reagan was, by any reasonable estimation, far more conservative than Nixon—he was more skeptical of government, more critical of Communism, and less interested in securing the goodwill of liberal opinion makers than was Nixon.

It was Buckley's best judgment that political conservatism could not survive another Goldwater-sized drubbing and that Nixon could pull the election off—and he did. Though Nixon beat Johnson's vice president Hubert Humphrey by less than a percentage of the popular vote, he won where it counted, and third-party candidate George Wallace won the Deep South, taking 46 electors. That made for a lopsided electoral college victory of 301 to 191.

So only four years after Barry Goldwater had lost in a landslide, conservatives could take some solace in the fact that LBJ's vice president suffered a humiliating defeat. Whether conservatism could survive Nixon was a different question.

ASHBROOK'S THE ONE

Nixon didn't leave Buckley's support for him unrewarded. He gave Buckley a post on the advisory board of the United States Information Agency, and he appointed him as a delegate to the United Nations, a position that Buckley turned into the book *A Delegate's Odyssey*. He also supported Bill's brother Jim, against a Republican challenger, in Jim's successful bid on the New York Conservative Party ticket to become a U.S. senator.

It is undeniable that Nixon's attention to Buckley had an effect, and Buckley didn't try to deny it. He told *Playboy* that he had discovered "a new sensual treat," which was to "have the President of the United States take notes while you are speaking to him." And: "It's always a little more difficult to be rhetorically ruthless with someone with whom you spend time." The magazine asked a pretty good follow-up question:

> PLAYBOY: Is Nixon conservative enough for you?
> BUCKLEY: My ideal conservative president would be one who would strike out for certain radical reforms that, in my judgment, would greatly benefit America and augment human freedom. But such a president cannot be elected—at this time—and couldn't get his program through Congress.[1]

So Buckley tried to give Nixon the benefit of the doubt, where possible, but ultimately found that it wasn't. On domestic policy Nixon went along with many liberal initiatives and dreamed up new ones—including affirmative action, the Environmental Protection Agency, and wage and price controls. On foreign policy he was, well, tricky. He derecognized Taiwan and recognized China. He stepped up the Vietnam War and then effectively sued for peace.

In his book *Overdrive*, Buckley recounted the story of why the *Boston Globe* stopped carrying his column. In the late 1970s the paper brought on a new editorial pages editor who had called Buckley a "cheap Jack careerist" who "spent so much time trying to justify the Nixon administration."

Buckley objected with a bill of particulars:

In August 1971 I convened an influential group in New York City which issued a statement publicly suspending our support of Nixon (front page, *New York Times*). In December 1971 I announced my support for the maverick candidacy of John Ashbrook against Richard Nixon. In February of 1972 I alone (I think) of the seventy reporters following Nixon in China categorically criticized Nixon's behavior, and the Shanghai Communique. In March of 1972 I declined in a personal letter to Nixon reappointment as a member of the U.S. Advisory Commission on Information.[2]

And he was just getting warmed up.

When Buckley was asked, in the fall of 1972, to make the case for Nixon, he instead chose to use his entire time ridiculing Democratic nominee George McGovern. McGovern was doing so badly in the polls, Buckley mocked, that it was not even certain he would "get the votes of Bob & Ted & Carol & Alice," and this in spite of the fact that he was "running against a president with the smallest personal constituency since James Buchanan's."[3]

Perhaps recognizing the trouble he had got himself into by allowing Nixon to draw him, however briefly, into his administration, when Ronald Reagan was elected president in 1980, Buckley preemptively turned down any appointments.

WATERGATE EXECUTOR

The public revelations of the Watergate burglary that came from the trials of the government-sponsored burglars did not surprise Bill Buckley one bit. He'd known for nearly a year of the revelations to come, though the way he had come to that knowledge created the sort of dilemma that most of us will face at one point.

It's much worse when such a thing happens to a journalist with regular access to camera crews. Buckley knew something important but had to pretend shock as events unfolded. He resorted to make-believe because of how he stumbled across that particular bit of intelligence.

Buckley wrote about this dilemma in *Nearer, My God* while

considering what it means to be a godparent. Technically, a godfather is supposed to look after the Catholic faith of his godsons and daughters. Practically, a godfather has no authority over the children, and so Buckley would instead send his godchildren small checks on their birthdays.

But in the case of Howard Hunt it was different. Hunt was Buckley's old boss from the CIA and one of the Nixon White House's "plumbers"—contract dirty tricks operatives—who had got caught breaking into the Democratic National Committee headquarters in the Watergate Hotel in June 1972.

On December 8, 1972, while the case of the Watergate burglary was winding its way through the courts, Hunt's wife, Dorothy, died in a plane crash. Buckley learned from the nightly news that he had been named executor of her will.

Not long after, "Howard came by with his second daughter (a godchild, whom I had never before laid eyes on) to my apartment in New York. In a few hours he recounted the entire story of Watergate." Hunt put Buckley "about nine months ahead of the news as, day by day, it would develop."

Buckley's old boss "knew that in a matter of months he'd be in jail, leaving his orphaned children, aged twenty-three, twenty, sixteen and seven, unchaperoned," and so turned to his former underling to help look after the well-being of his children. Bill and Pat Buckley did what they could to help Hunt's kids out.[4]

But that left Bill with the "professional problem" of what to do about Watergate, in light of the fact that he edited a magazine, wrote three columns a week, and hosted a regular television show that grappled with current events. Buckley saw the gathering storm in advance and tried to do what he could to get conservatives and the country ready for a new president.

He distanced himself from Nixon by speaking out more vigorously against the president's policies, calling for Nixon's resignation at the end of 1973, and encouraging Jim Buckley to call for Nixon's resignation in January 1974. Jim did so in March.

VICE-PRESIDENTIAL MATERIAL

When he finally had Vice President Gerald Ford as a guest on *Firing Line* in the summer of 1974, Buckley "attempted for a full hour to get the vice president to talk simply about the questions I had in mind," namely what might happen as the House of Representatives' impeachment vote loomed.

"I hardly succeeded," Buckley later lamented, because Ford had decided "that even to entertain the hypothetical possibility that Nixon would be impeached would suggest that he favored his impeachment."[5] Buckley was attempting to be kind to Ford, who—six weeks after the show aired—became America's thirty-eighth president.

Ford and Buckley should have been able to get along. During the 1950s Ford had worked to buck party leadership and install a younger, more conservative crop of representatives in positions of power. Though he would later acquire a reputation as a moderate Republican, he had proved more than happy to go along with many recent conservative crusades, including the push to impeach liberal Supreme Court justices.

But Ford was wrong-footed from the start of his sojourn in the White House. Conservatives could just about deal with his pardoning Nixon. What Ford called "our long national nightmare" was especially acute for those on the right. It caused heavy losses for Republicans in 1974, however, and Ford utterly failed to right things.

Ford had already started out in such a way that many conservatives were going to have a hard time warming to him. He had been appointed vice president when conservative favorite Spiro Agnew was forced out over construction kickbacks that he had taken while governor of Maryland. Ford then made things worse by appointing that old Republican liberal welterweight Nelson Rockefeller as his vice president, and further compounded the problem by refusing to meet with Nobel laureate and Russian dissident Aleksandr Solzhenitsyn for fear that it might offend the Soviets.

Enter Ronald Reagan. He challenged Ford in the Republican primaries in 1976 and fought it out all the way to the convention. Reagan lost the nomination that year; then Ford lost in the general election to a little-known Southern governor. It was a dispiriting defeat, but it cleared the way for the election, four years later, of a conservative president who was very close to Buckley's ideal.

10

QUEENS, SPIDERS, BUTTONS

When Bill Buckley was presented with a contract to write a novel in 1974, he wasn't sure he was up to it. He had gone out for lunch with Sam Vaughan, then an editor at Doubleday, and had made a passing comment that he'd recently read Fredrick Forsyth's spy novel *The Day of the Jackal* and might like at some point to try his hand at that sort of thing. The next day, Buckley came into the offices of *National Review* and found a book contract on his desk, waiting for his signature.

Buckley hesitated to sign it, for two reasons. He had never written fiction, and he had recently learned that a manuscript by former Nixon speechwriter and *New York Times* columnist William Safire had been rejected by his publisher, per the standard but rarely invoked "acceptable manuscript" clause in book contracts. (The book can comply with the contract in all other ways but still be rejected based on the publisher's best judgment.) Buckley suspected politics was behind the rejection, and he worried that his own politics could make things difficult in a new writing market.

So he struck a deal with Vaughan. The contract would be redrawn to specify that Buckley would produce about one hundred pages and show it to the publisher, who would then either greenlight the rest of the book or pay a kill fee. He needn't have worried. Buckley went to Gstaad, Switzerland, for the winter of 1974–75 and produced the sample pages and then the whole novel in about six weeks. The next year *Saving the Queen* hit bookstores. It was a commercial and critical success.

The central character in *Saving the Queen* and of Buckley's next nine novels was Blackford Oakes, a dashingly handsome Yale student from the class of 1951 (Buckley was class of 1950), a veteran of World War II who didn't want to get drafted into the Korean War, and, thus, a rookie recruit to the CIA. Much of Oakes's training was based on the training that Bill Buckley had actually received.

Buckley would try for the rest of his life to deny that Oakes was his fictional doppelganger—to little success. He protested to the *Paris Review* in 1996 that Oakes is an "engineer," a "Protestant," and "a pilot, which I was not." Oakes was also a career officer in the CIA, said Buckley, "and I'd quit after nine months." He did admit some similarities:

BUCKLEY: It is quite true that he's conservative. . . .

> And he's also pro-American. And we're both
> bright, sure.
> *PARIS REVIEW*: And you're both admirers of Bill
> Buckley.
> BUCKLEY: Exactly![1]

Both Oakes and Buckley came from conservative families
with prewar isolationist politics. Both were educated during
their teens in English boarding schools and had a rough time
of it. Both became dedicated anti-Communists who would do
whatever they possibly could to hurt the Soviet Union. Some
of the differences that Buckley played up were almost comi-
cal. Why, Oakes was an Anglican who eventually married a
Catholic, while Buckley was a WASPy Catholic who married
an Anglican. All the difference in the world.

It's true that Buckley wasn't a World War II pilot like
Oakes, but it's also true that he went in with a few Yalies during
their college years and bought a prop plane. He had to learn on
the fly—literally—how to navigate in the dark. Once he fell
asleep at the wheel and almost crashed the plane, and he finally
did crash and total it, landing it near his sister Maureen's school
for a visit.

Most of the differences boiled down to this: Oakes could do
what Buckley could not. "There's a little touch of James Bond
in his experiences, which there never was in mine," Buckley told
Paris Review. Though "idealistic, thinking man's James Bond"
might be a bit closer to the mark. In the first novel, Oakes not

only beds the Queen of England; he manages to convince a Communist mole to kill himself to save both Moscow and Her Royal Highness from embarrassment. Indeed, many of the best moments in the Blackford Oakes books feature not savage violence but brinksmanship.

OAKES, BLACKFORD OAKES

Oakes was different from Bond in a fundamental way. Bond was a dutiful servant of the British government who began as, essentially, a very smart contract killer. He had deeply felt ancestral attachments to crown and country but no overriding ideals.

This stark realism seeps into the opening of the first Bond novel, *Casino Royale*: "The scent and smoke and sweat of a casino are nauseating at three in the morning. Then the soul-erosion produced by high gambling—a compost of greed and fear and nervous tension—becomes unbearable and the senses awake and revolt from it. James Bond suddenly knew that he was tired."[2]

In contrast, Buckley immediately introduces us to an older Oakes who knows exactly what he's about. In 1975 the Senate established the Church Committee—nicknamed for its chairman, Idaho Democrat Frank Church—to look into the various activities of the CIA. Oakes refuses even to take the oath to testify in front of them in a closed-door session, for fear that his words will leak out. In one of those tricks of cozying up to the reader, *Saving the Queen* is one story from the past that Oakes manages not to tell them. The readers of *Saving the Queen* get the goods instead.

Over the next eighteen years, in nine more novels and then in a surprise late addition in 2005, Buckley told more of those stories. He called the first book an exercise in "literary iconoclasm," in which the Americans were clearly the good guys. He told the *Paris Review* that his Oakes books "are novels that *celebrate* the Cold War."

Buckley explained that in his adult lifetime "somewhere between fifty and sixty million people were killed *other* than as a result of war or pestilence, and in most cases . . . were the victims of the Communists." He complained that the Cold War was "the great political drama of the twentieth century, and there is extraordinarily little literature about it written in the novel form." He aimed to change that.

Buckley's goal in writing the Blackford Oakes novels was to entertain the reader but also to make a polemical point—which was that, for all their many faults and awful mistakes, America was doing the right thing in seeking to destroy organized Communism.

The books disdained "ambiguists" even while they showed how those people with moral objections sometimes had an absolutely irrefutable point. Oakes himself is often deeply troubled by the things that his government asks him to do—from the things it asks him to turn a blind eye to, to lies and betrayals that it orders. His longtime girlfriend Sally, a devout Catholic, first refuses to marry him and then ties the knot with another man precisely because she does not want to be with a man who is, in a sense, living a lie.

Buckley manages to get readers to side with the Americans in spite of all of this by showing us how much worse the Communists can be. It's not just the killing that stirs us to anger but the gestures that accompany it—hanging an idealistic student rebel and forbidding him to make the sign of the cross before he's killed; killing a helpless pregnant woman who is in surgery—that show what an utter lack of human decency Communism breeds. At least the Americans have the decency to see how indecent this all is, the books, in effect, argue. When Ronald Reagan orders . . . but we're getting ahead of ourselves.

KILL THE SPIDER

Bill Buckley entered the high point of his fame in 1977. It can be confidently dated because that's the year when the Woody Allen movie *Annie Hall* was released. The film is the story of a romance that goes sour between a neurotic left-wing comedian named Alvy and his girlfriend, Annie (played by Allen and Diane Keaton).

In the "spider scene," Annie asks Alvy to come over to her apartment to dispose of a "big black spider in the bathroom." He grouses, then asks for a magazine to use as a weapon. And he is shocked by her choice of literature:

ALVY: What is this? What are you—since when do you read the *National Review*? What are you turning into?

ANNIE: Well, I like to try to get all points of view.

ALVY: It's wonderful. Then why don'tcha get William F. Buckley to kill the spider?[3]

That isn't the only scene in the film that features a political magazine. At one point Alvy makes a joke. "I heard that *Commentary* and *Dissent* had merged and formed *Dysentery*," but he never names the editors of those distinguished journals.

MR. PRESIDENT . . .

According to old *National Review* hand Richard Brookhiser, Buckley harbored doubts that Ronald Reagan would be able to seize the Republican nomination in 1980, but he kept those to himself—mostly. Brookhiser even eavesdropped on one phone conversation in which Buckley was talking up Democrat Daniel Patrick Moynihan, the same brilliant liberal Nixon adviser and Cold Warrior who had bested his brother Jim for a senate seat in 1976.[4]

Buckley and Reagan had squared off in January, 1978, on *Firing Line* on opposite sides of what should be done with the Panama Canal. (Buckley was for giving it back to Panama. Reagan wanted to keep it.) Buckley in his introduction called Reagan "the politician in America I admire most." In his memoir *Right Time, Right Place*, Brookhiser calls that "debater's blarney, but also true."

And so, when Reagan taped an episode of *Firing Line* in January 1980, before anybody knew if he'd be able to get through the gauntlet of the Republican primaries, Buckley could have been expected to hedge his bets. He went all in.

He resolved to ask Reagan "very direct questions on the assumption not that he was a *candidate* for President, but that he *was* President," and that's what he did. After explaining the setup, Buckley referred to Reagan as "Mr. President" for the whole show "someone who, one year and one week later, was inaugurated President."

THE GREAT NEGOTIATOR

Buckley's final, posthumously published, book—so far—was *The Reagan I Knew*. In the foreword, son Christopher wrote of the merits of his dad's final effort that "Reagan was an elusive personality." So elusive that his official biographer Edmund Morris actually inserted a fictional character into his book "in an attempt to deconstruct his subject." But though the late president "tended, famously, to shy away from personal intimacy, I think it's entirely possible that Pup [Christopher's name for his father] may have gotten as close to him as one could."[5]

Several reviewers agreed. *Booklist* critic David Pitt wrote that the book is "quite deceptive" because it "appears to be a slight, even inconsequential chronicle of the author's long friendship with Ronald Reagan, told through correspondence between the two men and also between the author and Reagan's wife, Nancy." This correspondence "seems on the surface to be concerned almost entirely with mundane matters"; however, these worked to create a "revealing" dual portrait—of Reagan and of Buckley. Pitt wrote that if readers only skimmed the book, they would miss something important.[6]

Daniel McCarthy, reviewer for the *American Conservative*, agreed that the book was full of insights and more. McCarthy said that the book "could have been called *The Reagan I Didn't Know*, for after a 40-year friendship Buckley suddenly realized he had misjudged the man." Buckley had speechified in 1985 words to the effect that Reagan "would, if he had to, pull the nuclear trigger." Buckley decided, he wrote in his final book, that he was very wrong in inferring that about Reagan.[7]

Buckley borrowed words of Henry Kissinger to explain why President Reagan would not have responded to a Soviet nuclear first strike by unleashing the United States' full nuclear arsenal. "After all, what would be the point?" Kissinger asked.[8] Buckley also believed that Reagan was "almost certainly the nicest man who has ever occupied the White House," and nice guys don't push the button.

Buckley represented Reagan's reluctance to go nuclear as a new revelation, something that occurred to him only in the last months of his (Buckley's) life, but that's not what comes through from the letters. My sense is that Buckley knew that Reagan could never do it from early on. Reagan hated nuclear weapons and wanted desperately to find some way to end them or at least make them matter less, thus his much-ridiculed "Star Wars" program. But both men also knew that if the Soviets had any clue about Reagan's feelings, the United States would not be able to exploit its chief rival's growing brittleness.

So Buckley did everything he could to prop up the image of the United States and Reagan as just crazy enough to go through with it. In early 1983, the U.S. Conference of Catholic Bishops issued a letter warning against the dangers of nuclear war. On May 6, Buckley responded in a scheduled lecture at St. Mary's College in Maryland by challenging the bishops on theological grounds. He observed that there were "many prelates sitting in the front row" of the auditorium, and any "applause from them was formalistic."

The address was well summarized by historian Patrick Allitt. Buckley, said Allitt, "cautioned against a new era of appeasement, fearing that after forty years of holding out against communism the church was beginning to lose its stomach for the protracted cold war. He added that Christians must be willing to give up their lives even, if need be, in apocalyptic nuclear wars, mindful of Jesus' message that 'His Kingdom is not of this world,' rather than succumb to Soviet tyranny."[9]

Buckley seemed to be "afraid that the widespread Christian antiwar sentiment of the early 1980s bespoke a veneration of life as a supreme good in itself. For Christians who aspire to Christ's Kingdom, he believed, it should ever remain no more than a contingent good."

It was an impressive reflection, but I think the public assertion of the thing—a theological justification for the popular slogan "better dead than red"—was far more important than whether it could survive sustained scrutiny. Buckley urged us to be ready for the end, and then praised the man who could hasten it. Here's a question for the ages: Was he bluffing?

11

EXIT STAGE RIGHT

Reagan was close to Buckley's ideal president for several reasons, one of which was that the former actor and California governor had been a charter subscriber of *National Review*. Reagan was a fusionist conservative, a pro-lifer, and a dedicated anti-Communist. He tried to cut taxes and regulation, rein in government spending, and build up the military so that the U.S. government could have more flexibility in dealing with the USSR.

Reagan pulled off some of that. He slashed top marginal tax rates and slowed down the growth of government, though—he lamented in his farewell address—not nearly enough. He had been thought of as a dangerous warmonger, but there were no large wars on his watch.

The marines were sent into Lebanon and then quickly yanked out. The invasion and toppling of the Marxist government of the Caribbean island nation of Grenada in 1983, code-named Operation Urgent Fury, went off almost without a hitch. It was a small pinprick that challenged the idea, the so-called Brezhnev Doctrine, that Communist revolutions were permanent.

The Iran-Contra scandal—arms had been sold to Iran to encourage the release of U.S. hostages, and those monies had been used to fund anti-Communist Nicaraguan rebels—was more controversial. But, really, it was one of many examples of Reagan's quiet but insistent support for rebels who wanted to fight off Communist governments. He also greatly increased support to indigenous rebels in Afghanistan, whose persistence and sure aim eventually forced the Russian army to withdraw in disgrace.

Buckley forcefully criticized Reagan in the 1980s over Reagan's nuclear arms reduction talks with Soviet president Mikhail Gorbachev and Reagan's offer to share Strategic Defense Initiative "Star Wars" antimissile technology with the Russians once America got it up and running.

These concessions had struck Buckley as extremely unwise, but he said his piece and ultimately trusted that Reagan would do the right thing. He believed in Reagan because of what Reagan believed. The USSR, Reagan publicly declared, in defiance of all the diplomatic censors, was an "evil empire," and he didn't just throw around words like *evil*.

Buckley was insistent that the heat should be kept on the Soviet Union because one flaw he thought he had discovered in Communism was that it had to produce a socialist heaven *on earth*, and a serious nuclear exchange would make that impossible. Since Christians do believe in an afterlife and do not need an earth in order to reach Paradise, and since most Americans are professing Christians of one stripe or another, he believed the threat of nukes could be the ultimate trump card. "How blessed we are that the Bolsheviks so specifically reject God!" he said at St. Mary's.

Put another way, Buckley believed that in any game of geopolitical chicken, the Soviets would have no choice but to swerve. Their secular faith was riding on it. He might have been right about it, though I, for one, am glad that we never found out. Buckley also believed that other measures short of that would contribute to Communism's downfall, and he was more than happy to back a president who worked to frustrate Soviet ambitions.

SUCCESSION PLANS

Buckley backed fellow Yalie and vice president George H. W. Bush in 1988, and he announced his retirement as editor in chief of *National Review* in 1990. Neither of those choices has aged well.

Bush proved to be a competent but uninspiring president. He oversaw the transition from the Communist to the post-Communist world. He won a crushing victory in Iraq. And then he lost in his reelection bid to a little-known Southern governor. (Maybe there's a historical pattern here . . .) He also enraged conservatives for a whole number of reasons—from raising taxes to disappointing pro-lifers.

Buckley handed *National Review* into the capable hands of veteran British journalist John O'Sullivan, but he never really let go. From the reader's point of view, he was about as big a presence in the magazine as he had ever been, and he retained all voting stock in the company.

For years before O'Sullivan, the magazine had been pushed and pulled by competing factions, and Buckley had kept the peace between them by keeping himself in charge. He was especially suited for the job because he loved the back and forth of debate, and he was a great synthesizer. He could take arguments from rival conservative factions and combine them in such a way that made all sides think they were getting something out of the deal. That was the grand bargain behind fusionism.

Buckley used other tricks to hold things together. His sister Priscilla was the longtime managing editor. The editorial policy of the magazine allowed any senior editor to publicly dissent from Buckley or the magazine, in the pages of *National Review*. He told a young Richard Brookhiser that Brookhiser would one day be editor in chief but asked that it be kept strictly under wraps. When he rescinded that offer, Buckley discouraged further discussion.

O'Sullivan didn't have the same resources as Buckley, which created problems. He brought on or regularly published several writers who wanted to change the magazine's and conservatism's stance on immigration. Reaganites had been broadly supportive of immigration, but this new crop of writers marshaled new evidence and arguments for why essentially unchecked immigration was a bad thing for America's fiscal health and culture.

This led to predictable clashes among conservatives, libertarians, and other members of the right-wing coalition. O'Sullivan wasn't as adept at mollifying aggrieved parties as was Buckley, and in 1996 Buckley fired him. He replaced O'Sullivan with a dark horse candidate, Rich Lowry, a one-time staff writer who would eventually consolidate his control over the whole *National Review* enterprise.

LUKEWARM WAR

The fact that O'Sullivan got anywhere, however, was evidence of Buckley's wish to rethink things a bit after the end of the Cold War. Many conservatives didn't alter their thinking substantially after the USSR dissolved. They still wanted a large military, U.S. dominance, and Ronald Reagan. When any new threat or irritation cropped up, they simply looked at it through the old Cold War goggles.

Buckley took a different approach. At his urging *National Review* came out in favor of drug legalization. In a public debate with Jesse Jackson, Buckley distinguished between that which should be "legal" and that which is "honorable." Obviously people should want what is honorable, but the law should not always compel it, argued the old fusionist. For instance, it should be legal to cast a ballot for Jesse Jackson, but Buckley said that certainly wasn't honorable. Jackson was not amused.[1]

Buckley also took some baby steps away from the foreign policy advice of many hawkish conservatives. He said that America should certainly be a great military power, and he supported the First Gulf War, but he rejected the progressive "Wilsonian" approach to foreign policy, which seeks above all else to make the world safe for democracy. Several conservatives beat the drums against China in the early 2000s. Buckley wasn't one of them.

He cautioned conservatives that in a post–Cold War world they should be wary of some of the arguments that they make to argue for interventionism because, after all, they would stumble upon a war soon enough that they would want to oppose. Many American conservatives opposed the 1998 Kosovo War, and after some initial words in favor of the intervention, Buckley joined them.

After initially supporting a return trip, he also denounced the 2003 invasion of Iraq. Buckley argued that the lack of weapons of mass destruction proved the opponents of the war had been right. He said that if America were a parliamentary democracy, the choice of war and its mismanagement would have cost Prime Minister George W. Bush his job. He supported a military surge as a way of salvaging something from an awful and—in his opinion, unnecessary—situation.

He wasn't completely untouched by the attacks of September 11, 2001. He was, of course, all for invading Afghanistan and crushing al-Qaeda and similar Islamic terrorist groups, but he had some skepticism for a broader war on terror, and that skepticism grew over time.

In 2005 Buckley published a surprise eleventh Blackford Oakes novel, with an end that made the end of novel ten, *A Very Private Plot*, impossible. In *A Very Private Plot*, Oakes finds himself in a pickle in the mid-1990s. As with *Saving the Queen*, he is asked to testify before Congress. The second time the Senate won't let him get away with refusing to swear an oath. *Last Call for Blackford Oakes* (spoiler warning) gets him out of that pickle by killing off Oakes in a gunfight—in 1989.

Buckley's research assistant for that book, Jaime Sneider, told me that when he was plotting out the novel, Buckley rejected all suggestions that Oakes should be taken out of mothballs and inserted into the war on terror. He would bury Oakes in the great struggle of the twentieth century, perhaps to keep future imitators from dragging him into a struggle that Buckley thought more dubious.[2]

Then there's the nuclear weapon business. In his final book Buckley wrote that he had changed his mind. Ronald Reagan wouldn't have pushed the button, even after a nuclear strike by the Soviets. Set aside for a moment whether Buckley actually changed his mind or simply revealed what he had known for some time. The reason that he spelled out his judgment is what matters.

Buckley wrote that his change of mind should perfect how future generations think of nuclear deterrence. Maybe it worked with the Soviets, but that was due to the specific beliefs of Marxism. And if a nuclear deterrent is ineffective, he argued, then it's almost certainly immoral, and we should come up with other ways of securing the peace of nations that do not involve the real promise of Armageddon.

He suggested that if a "non-ambiguist" like Ronald Reagan wouldn't do it, or if a vicious real politicker like Henry Kissinger wouldn't advise any president to push the button, then no U.S. president ever would again. What that would mean for the future of the world is uncertain, but one good possibility—and I'm speculating here—was that in the fullness of time, the United States should pound its nuclear swords into clean energy plowshares and not play such an outsized role in world affairs.

NO ALTERNATIVE

The last decade or so of Buckley's life was largely about discharging obligations. *Nearer, My God*, his book about Catholicism, appeared in 1997. It was not an easy book to write. He started writing it, then stopped, then plowed through, because—he suggested in interviews—he owed it to God. The result was an entertaining, digressive consideration of the faith. Buckley folded *Firing Line* in 1999, after more than fifteen hundred episodes, because he didn't "want to die onstage."

And in 2004, at the age of seventy-nine, Bill Buckley finally relinquished ownership of *National Review* to a board of trustees, including his son Christopher and Rich Lowry. Deborah

Solomon, interrogator of the *New York Times Magazine*'s weekly Questions For column, interviewed Buckley about that transfer and, if the published transcript is a good guide, he was as impossible as ever.

Solomon tried most of her journalistic tricks, including flattery and appeals to Buckley's supposed snobbery. She opened by calling Buckley a "high IQ conservative." She agreed with recent criticisms of the architects of the Iraq War. ("Their ambitions . . . do seem to be leading to their self destruction," Solomon opined.)

The role she was trying to get him to play was the conservative critic of conservatism. Other than one dig each at George W. Bush and neoconservatives ("they simply overrate the reach of U.S. power and influence"), Buckley didn't bite. So she circled back to his more controversial statements:

SOLOMON: In the 50's, you famously claimed that whites were culturally superior to African Americans.

BUCKLEY: The point I made about white cultural supremacy was sociological. It reflected, in a different but complementary context, the postulates of the National Association for the Advancement of Colored People.

SOLOMON: What are you talking about?

BUCKLEY: The call for the "advancement" of colored people presupposes they are behind. Which they were, in 1958, by any standards of measurement.

And:

> SOLOMON: Do you regret saying that patients with
> AIDS should be tattooed on their backsides to
> identify them to potential bedmates?
> BUCKLEY: If the protocol had been accepted, many
> who caught the infection unguardedly would be
> alive. Probably over a million.[3]

His answers led her to call him "indifferent to suffering," and he
certainly proved indifferent to her criticism. He said that his health
was "infirm, though nothing terminal or unique." He supposed
that he had at some point cheated on his taxes because these days
"it's impossible to not cheat on your taxes." The ideal tax rate
would be "as much, but not more, than your neighbors pay."

Buckley shrugged off a question about whether his son and
new *National Review* trustee Christopher was as conservative as
his pop by saying, "It would be rude of me to inquire." Solomon
then threw a minor fit. "Must you be so clever at all times?" she
asked. "I haven't practiced the alternative," he explained.

Buckley held on to his wit until the end, but in his declining
years, and especially after the surprise death of his wife, Pat, to
a botched surgery in April 2007, a certain morbidity crept in,
and he didn't care who knew it. He sold a boat in 2004 and said
that he was preparing for a different sort of voyage. And he
said, in an appearance on the *Charlie Rose Show*, that he wanted
to die, that if a pill was invented that could extend one's life by

twenty-five years or so, he wouldn't take it. He was tired of this life and ready for something different.

STILL FAMOUS

William F. Buckley Jr. was found dead on February 27, 2008. His body was slumped over his desk in the sprawling garage-office of his Stamford, Connecticut, home.

His health had been failing for some time from emphysema and assorted hazards of old age as he worked to finish one last book about his old friend Ronald Reagan. It was rumored that he had not got far enough along for an editor to come along and posthumously stitch something together, but those worries proved to be unfounded. Buckley's final labor, *The Reagan I Knew*, was released that October.

In the foreword, son Christopher explained that "one might suppose" this was his father's final book, but you never know. There may be more essay collections, and there are likely a few manuscripts spirited away that could be turned into books. The interest is certainly there.

The funeral Mass was held at St. Patrick's Cathedral in Manhattan on April 4. Christopher told the gathered crowd of thousands, "We talked about this day, he and I. He said, 'If I'm still famous, try to get the cardinal to do the service at St. Patrick's. If I'm not, just tuck me away in Stamford.'" He waited two beats, surveying the crowd, and added, "Well, Pop, I guess you're still famous."

American Spectator crack reporter Shawn Macomber attended that funeral and did a wonderful job describing the scene. He quoted one headline "Rich, Famous Wish Multi-Talented William F. Buckley Farewell" and explained that "these luminaries were but pinpricks in a tapestry of more than two thousand ordinary people, many of whom had traveled great distances to pay their respects and, often as not, proudly announce, with little prompting and a hint of the desire to testify, the year they first discovered *National Review* and how profound its impact was on them. (It was, invariably, *profound*.)"

"Apropos of nothing," wrote Macomber, "a man related to me on the church steps that Buckley's writings on religion had turned the tide of his agnostic mind toward belief—and then took great pains to insist he was not at all alone in this experience."[4]

Appendix

RECOMMENDED READING

Whenpeople say to me that they have read a few of William F. Buckley Jr.'s columns and articles but not his books and want to know where they should start, this presents a dilemma. Buckley wrote so much about so many different subjects that there is no logical go-to first book.

I could tell them to read Buckley's first book, *God and Man at Yale*, but Buckley himself eventually did not think too highly of that book. He thought the point had been worth making, but he winced at some of the writing. *Up from Liberalism* is a good introduction to Buckley's skill at peeling liberal arguments like onions, but most of the controversies are extremely dated. The modern reader can only get so worked up about Eleanor Roosevelt. Buckley wrote several books about sailing, and a moving article about selling his boat, but if sailing isn't your bag—and it is not mine—then that's probably not the best point of entry.

So let's try this. If you are interested in Buckley's life, then start with *Miles Gone By*. It's a collection of previously published essays about his life and his friends. Buckley took great care in the selection of those essays, knowing that this was the closest he would ever come to writing a formal autobiography. Then look at the books that paint a snapshot of his life. *The Unmaking of a Mayor* documents the youngish media figure coming into his own in the crazy 1960s. *Cruising Speed* captures a week in the life of Buckley in the '70s. And in *Overdrive* we see an almost-old man, still hard going in the '80s.

For biography, as opposed to autobiography, start with John Judis's *William F. Buckley, Jr.: Patron Saint of the Conservatives*. Judis's politics are not Buckley's, but it is an undeniably good biography. Mark Royden Winchell wrote a series of interpretive essays titled *William F. Buckley Jr.* for Twayne's United States Authors Series. Brother Reid wrote up a perfectly good set of reminiscences about Bill and the rest of the clan, called *An American Family*. And the conservative historian Lee Edwards has written a book that I have not set eyes on but am confident will be a good read, *William F. Buckley, Jr.: The Maker of a Movement*.

If you are interested in the arguments that defined Buckley's life, start with his collection of speeches, *Let Us Talk of Many Things*, and his column collections. My personal favorite collection would have to be *The Jeweler's Eye*. For a more extended treatment of Buckley on McCarthyism, read *McCarthy and His Enemies* and *The Redhunter*. For the infamous *Mater et Magistra* controversy, read Garry Wills's *Politics and Catholic Freedom*. For Buckley's take on objectivism, read his novel *Getting It Right*.

As for Buckley's fiction, my personal favorite novel was his first non–Blackford Oakes novel, *Brothers No More*, about a monstrous war hero and a heroic coward. Also, his one practically unheard-of children's book, *The Temptation of Wilfred Malachey*, isn't half bad. But that's not why you're here, right?

If you want to wade into the Blackford Oakes novels—and you *should*—start with *Saving the Queen* and stick around for the second novel, *Stained Glass*, which won an American Book Award. Then feel free to skip around a bit and skim. Remember what I noted in the last chapter, that the set-up for book number 10, *A Very Private Plot*, and number 11, *Last Call for Blackford Oakes*, are incompatible. Every Oakes novel featured one long character sketch. The first ten of those sketches are collected in the *Blackford Oakes Reader*.

For a bigger picture of the conservative movement that Buckley did so much to found, read George Nash's *The Conservative Intellectual Movement in America Since 1945* and two books by Patrick Allitt, *The Conservatives* and *Catholic Intellectuals and Conservative Politics in America, 1950–1985*.

For more on the religious thought of Buckley, read *Nearer, My God* and read his columns, both collected and not. Especially later in life, there remained a sharpness in those columns that dealt with faith, because he remained certain that was the one thing he could take with him.

NOTES

Introduction

1. George Nash, "Simply Superlative," *National Review Online*, February 28, 2008, http://article.nationalreview.com/349852/simply-superlative/george-h-nash.
2. Patrick Allitt, *The Conservatives: Ideas & Personalities Throughout American History* (New Haven, CT: Yale University Press, 2009), 175.
3. Quoted in William F. Buckley Jr., *The Reagan I Knew* (New York: Basic Books, 2008), xii.
4. 2 Chronicles 18, author's paraphrase.
5. Mark Stricherz, "Buckley Wasn't a 'Conservative' Catholic," *Get Religion*, February 28, 2008, http://www.getreligion.org/?p=3225.
6. Anthony Stevens-Arroyo, "WFB: The Primordial Cafeteria Catholic," *On Faith*, August 14, 2008, http://newsweek.washington-post.com/onfaith/catholicamerica/2008/08/wfb_jr_the_primordial_cafeteri.html.

Chapter 1

1. William F. Buckley Jr., *Miles Gone By: A Literary Autobiography* (Washington DC: Regnery, 2004), 48–50.
2. Pope Pius XI, "Iniquis Afflictisque," November 18, 1926, http://

www.vatican.va/holy_father/pius_xi/encyclicals/documents/hf_p-xi_enc_18111926_iniquis-afflictisque_en.html.

3. *Firing Line*, June 26, 2009, http://www.youtube.com/watch?v=h4ypqCYPduI.

4. Buckley, *Miles Gone By*, 1–9.

5. Reid Buckley, *An American Family: The Buckleys* (New York: Threshold, 2008), 13–14.

6. Christopher Matthews, *Kennedy and Nixon: The Rivalry That Shaped Postwar America* (New York: Simon & Schuster, 1996), 75.

7. Buckley, *Miles Gone By*, 1–9.

8. William F. Buckley Jr. "Aloise Steiner Buckley: An Epilogue" in *Nearer, My God: An Autobiography of Faith* (Orlando: Harcourt, 1997), 277–86.

9. Garry Wills, "Daredevil," *Atlantic*, July/August 2009.

10. Joe Queenan, *Closing Time: A Memoir* (New York: Viking, 2009), 157.

11. Buckley, *Nearer, My God*, 277–86.

CHAPTER 2

1. This chapter draws extensively on the introduction to the 25th anniversary edition.

2. McGeorge Bundy, "The Attack on Yale," *Atlantic Monthly*, November 1951, http://www.theatlantic.com/magazine/archive/1969/12/the-attack-on-yale/6724/.

3. Author interview.

4. Judy Wang, "Constitution Burned in Div. School Protests: Divinity students burned Ten Commandments, Bill of Rights at Ash Wed. service," *Yale Daily News*, March 6, 2007, http://www.yaledailynews.com/news/scitech-news/2007/03/06/constitution-burned-in-div-school-protest/.

5. Brooks Mather Kelly, *Yale: A History* (New Haven, CT: Yale University Press, 1999), 31.

CHAPTER 3

1. William F. Buckley Jr., "Who Did What?" *National Review Online*, November 1, 2005, http://old.nationalreview.com/buckley/buckley200511011324.asp.

2. Whittaker Chambers, *Odyssey of a Friend: Letters to William F. Buckley, Jr.: 1954–1961* (New York: Putnam, 1969), 47–49.

3. Jeffrey Hart, *When the Going Was Good: American Life in the Fifties* (New York: Crown, 1982), 122–23.

4. William F. Buckley Jr. and L. Brent Bozell, *McCarthy and His Enemies: The Record and Its Meaning* (Washington DC: Regnery, 1954), 335.

5. Mark Royden Winchell, *William F. Buckley Jr.* (Twayne's United States authors series, 1984), 24.

6. William F. Buckley Jr., *Up from Liberalism* (Hillman Books, 1961), 26–29.

7. Clark Judge, "Remarks to the Portsmouth Institute," June 20, 2009.

CHAPTER 4

1. Lee Edwards, "WFB: A Catholic with All Flags Unfurled," delivered to the Portsmouth Institute, June 20, 2009.

2. John Le Carre, *The Spy Who Came in from the Cold* (Great Britain: Victor Gollancz, 1963), 31.

3. Eric Pfeiffer, "Back to the Future," *National Review Online*, February 24, 2005, http://old.nationalreview.com/beltway/056949.html.

4. "Our Mission Statement," *National Review*, November 19, 1955.

5. William F. Buckley Jr., *Flying High: Remembering Barry Goldwater* (New York: Basic Books, 2008), 35–38.

6. William F. Buckley Jr., "In the End, We Will Bury Him," in *Let Us Talk of Many Things: The Collected Speeches* (New York: Forum, 2000), 33–38.

CHAPTER 5

1. Whittaker Chambers, *Witness* (New York: Random House, 1952), 9.

2. Niels Bjerre-Poulsen, *Right Face: Organizing the American Conservative Movement 1945–1965* (Copenhagen: Museum Tusculanum Press, 2003), 193.

3. George Scialabba, *What Are Intellectuals Good For?* (Boston: Pressed Wafer, 2009), 137–46.

4. Buckley, *Flying High*, ix.

5. Lee Edwards, "The Conservative Consensus: Frank Meyer, Barry

Goldwater, and the Politics of Fusionism" (Heritage Foundation First Principles #8), January 22, 2007, http://www.heritage.org/research/nationalsecurity/fp8.cfm.

6. Barry Goldwater, *Conscience of a Conservative* (New York: Hillman, 1960), 67.

7. Crispin Sartwell, *Extreme Virtue: Truth and Leadership in Five Great American Lives* (Albany, NY: SUNY Press, 2003), 63–88.

8. Buckley, *Let Us Talk of Many Things*, 74–77.

9. Ronald Reagan, "A Time for Choosing," October 27, 1964, http://www.reagan.utexas.edu/archives/reference/timechoosing.html.

CHAPTER 6

1. Most quotes in this chapter are from William F. Buckley Jr., *The Unmaking of a Mayor* (New York: Viking, 1966).

2. Author's edit.

3. Author interview.

CHAPTER 7

1. William F. Buckley Jr., "James Lane Buckley," in *Inveighing We Will Go* (New York: Putnam, 1972), 340–45.

2. Buckley, *The Unmaking of a Mayor*, 1–6.

3. William F. Buckley Jr., *On the Firing Line: The Public Life of Private Figures* (New York: Random House, 1989), 5.

4. Author interview.

5. Buckley, *On the Firing Line*, 93–97.

6. Michael Kimmage, in *A New Literary History of America* (Cambridge: Belknap Press, 2009), 948–52.

7. Buckley, *Inveighing We Will Go*, 19–64.

8. Damian Kearney, "Some Recollections of William F. Buckley at Yale and Portsmouth," June 20, 2009.

CHAPTER 8

1. "Why the South Must Prevail," *National Review*, August 24, 1957.

2. John B. Judis, *William F. Buckley, Jr.: Patron Saint of the Conservatives* (New York: Simon & Schuster), 138–39.

3. "Editorial Clarification," *National Review*, September 7, 1957.

4. Buckley, *On the Firing Line*, 161–66.

5. William F. Buckley Jr., "The Resistance of Black Leaders," in *Happy Days Were Here Again: Reflections of a Libertarian Journalist* (Holbrook, MA: Adams Publishing, 1993), 129.

6. The controversy is recounted, in detail, here: Garry Wills, *Politics & Catholic Freedom* (Washington DC: Regnery, 1964), 1–20.

7. Buckley, *On the Firing Line*, xxxvii.

8. William F. Buckley Jr., syndicated column, March 19, 1966.

9. William F. Buckley Jr., "Ayn Rand: R.I.P." *National Review*, April 2, 1982.

10. Whittaker Chambers, "Big Sister Is Watching," *National Review*, December 28, 1957, http://old.nationalreview.com/flashback/flashback200501050715.asp.

11. Michael Harrington, "Suddenly the Tories are asking: Who is John Galt? The answer is: bad news," *The Spectator*, August 17, 2002.

Chapter 9

1. Buckley, *Inveighing We Will Go*, 33.

2. William F. Buckley Jr., *Overdrive* (Boston: Little Brown, 1981), 195–202.

3. Buckley, *Let Us Talk of Many Things*, 202–07.

4. Buckley, *Nearer, My God*, (1997), 217–21.

5. Buckley, *On the Firing Line*, 149–150.

Chapter 10

1. "The Art of Fiction No. 146," *The Paris Review*, summer 1996, http://www.parisreview.com/viewinterview.php/prmMID/1395.

2. Ian Fleming, *Casino Royale* (Great Britain: Jonathan Cape, 1953), 1.

3. Woody Allen, *Annie Hall*, 1977.

4. Richard Brookhiser, *Right Time, Right Place: Coming of Age with William F. Buckley, Jr., and the Conservative Movement* (New York: Basic Books, 2009), 84.

5. Christopher Buckley, in Buckley, *The Reagan I Knew*, xii (foreword).

6. David Pitt, review, *Booklist*, November 1, 2008.

7. Daniel McCarthy, "Getting Reagan Right," *American Conservative*, January 26, 2009.

8. Buckley Jr., *The Reagan I Knew*, 178.

9. Patrick Allitt, *Catholic Intellectuals and Conservative Politics in America, 1950–1985* (Ithaca, NY: Cornell University Press, 1993), 289–306.

CHAPTER 11

1. Oh, just watch the YouTube video: http://www.youtube.com/watch?v=2BbmbIoynZQ.

2. Author interview.

3. "Conservatively Speaking: Questions for William F. Buckley, Jr.," *New York Times Magazine*, July 11, 2004, http://www.nytimes.com/2004/07/11/magazine/11QUESTIONS.html?pagewanted=1.

4. Shawn Macomber, "Mourning in St. Patrick's," *American Spectator*, April 7, 2008, http://spectator.org/archives/2008/04/07/mourning-in-st-patricks.

ACKNOWLEDGMENTS

Many thanks are owed to my publisher, Joel Miller, for the contract and encouragement, to the beautiful and patient Kristen Parrish, for her editorial suggestions, and to crack proofreader Janene MacIvor, for rescuing this manuscript from countless misspellings and typos. (In the most egregious instance, I had somehow managed to misspell Whittaker Chambers's first name as "Whattaker.") Thanks to my old friend and confidant W. James Antle III, for remembering that bit about Huey Newton. Thanks to Helen Rittelmeyer, for her invaluable research assistance. Thanks to Sean Higgins, Al Canata, William Yeatman, Erica Morbeck, and Vinnie Vernuccio, for their encouragement. Thanks to Ramesh Ponnuru, Robert VerBruggen, and Neal Freeman, for filling in some gaps. Thanks to Wlady Pleszczynski, John Wilson, and Russ Smith, for publishing some of my preliminary thoughts about Buckley. Thanks to several folks at Capital Research

Center: to Terry Scanlon for the time away to write this, to Robert Huberty for his library and his liberality, to Matthew Vadum for making me laugh, to Gordon Cummings for the trips to McDonald's, to Chris Krukewitt for the actuarial acrobatics, to Jana Erwin for the popcorn, and to Brent "Bread" Jordan for putting up with us. Thanks, finally, to Bob Lott, my father and write-in candidate for the presidency in the 2008 elections. And, yes, had he won, I'm quite certain he would have demanded a recount.